A 50-DAY DEVOTIONAL

BASED ON THE
THEATRICAL LIVE
EXPERIENCE

THE THORN

SO LOVED

Finding your place in
God's epic story

JOHN BOLIN

BroadStreet
PUBLISHING

BroadStreet Publishing Group, LLC
Racine, Wisconsin, USA
BroadStreetPublishing.com

SO LOVED
Finding Your Place in God's Epic Story

ISBN-13: 978-1-4245-5203-0 (hardcover)
ISBN-13: 978-1-4245-5225-2 (e-book)

Author represented by Alive Literary Agency, 7680 Goddard Street, Suite 200, Colorado Springs, Colorado 80920, www.aliveliterary.com.

Cover design by Chris Garborg at garborgdesign.com
Interior design & typesetting by Kimberly Sagmiller at fudgecreative.com

Printed in China
16 17 18 19 20 5 4 3 2 1

CONTENTS

DEDICATION

For my kids—five of the best chapters of my story:
Harrison, Chandler, Katherine, Alison, and Tate.

ACKNOWLEDGEMENTS

EVERY STORY HAS A CAST OF CHAR-ACTERS, and without them, the story would never happen at all. This book has been no different. Beginning with my best friend and wife, Sarah. I am better because of her and so is this book. Thank you for enduring hours of reading and rereading and for your special contribution of the chapter Suffering. Thanks to everyone at Alive Communications for believing in this project, especially Rick Christian, who has walked with me from fly fishing to kingdom fishing. Lisa Jackson, you are an agent extraordinaire and kept me on the rails when I needed it most. Thanks to my new friends at BroadStreet Publishing. Carlton Garborg for taking a risk and David Sluka for being a champion and working ideas until they landed. Thanks also to Bill Watkins, whose editorial hand saw this over the finish line. To my friend and co-laborer at The Thorn, Andrew Harmon—thank you for helping me make every chapter better, and thank you especially for the chapter you added, Sand. Katie Schmidt, your love for words and God's story is obvious. Thanks to the others who read this and made it better: all of our incredible Thorn Conservatory students, my staff, and my parents, Rod and Vija. Finally, a special thank-you to Tom and Lori Forster for your endless generosity and for letting me camp out in your condo to get this done. There's something special about that place. Love to all of the cast and crew and attendees of The Thorn over all these years. Without you, there wouldn't be a book at all.

DAY 1

STORY

WELCOME TO THE STORY

EVERYONE HAS A STORY.

But life stories are not as simple as we sometimes make them out to be. They are messy and complicated. They have layers and twists and turns that are known only by the ones who live them, and even then only up to the moment.

Every person you see—at the grocery store, at the movies, driving in their cars on the freeway and fiddling with their radios or cell phones—every one of them has a story that is unlike anyone else's. They have their own childhood memories, their own dreams, and their own fears. Each story has a different beginning and a different middle and will have a different ending. Ironically, as varied as the details are, story is one of the few things we all have in common.

As someone who earns his living as a storyteller, I think about this a lot.

Have you ever noticed that some movies stick with you long after the film is over, gnawing at some deep part of you, as if the movie had been made just for you, to tell you something?

Good stories do that. They create worlds that in many ways reflect our own. I think that's part of the reason some movies and books and plays haunt us while others are simply entertainment. A good story stirs the soul at the deepest level because it's a picture of the human experience and a reflection of the much bigger story of God.

The story of God goes back to the beginning of time and weaves its way through history, pausing at the climactic moment of Jesus' death and resurrection and then continuing on to this moment as you read these words. The story of God is all at once mysterious, adventurous, tragic, and wonderful. It is the most epic narrative ever told.

And the Author wants to invite you into it.

When Jesus stood at the Sea of Galilee with one of His top recruits, a gnarly fisherman named Peter, He invited Peter into His story by simply saying, "Follow Me" (Matthew 4:18–20 ESV). Jesus didn't ask Peter to recite a pledge or change anything about himself. He didn't have him sign a waiver or learn a secret handshake or throw away his Bob Dylan albums. He simply asked Peter to go along with Him, to join His story. Peter didn't need to think about it for very long. I imagine that he sort of shrugged his shoulders and said, "OK, I'm in."

That was Peter's big conversion. That moment when he decided to follow Jesus, to step out of a boat and into the story of God that was already happening around him. From that time on, Peter's story was interwoven with Jesus' story. It wasn't always pretty, but it was beautiful.

I think sometimes we overcomplicate what it means to follow Jesus. Now, that's not to say that following Jesus is simple or trite or comfortable. Far from it. But I love the idea of stepping into God's story. For me, that's a lot better than stepping into the stuff of religion.

I'm not a theologian. I'm a storyteller. Twenty years ago, while I was working as a youth pastor, I created an "illustrated sermon" as a way to show high school students that Jesus *so loved* them that He was willing to give His life for them so that they could truly live. It was basically a passion play on steroids. That illustrated sermon became known as "The Thorn," and the title has stuck for the past two decades as I've taken that story across the world.

If you've seen "The Thorn," this book will help you dig deeper into the pages of the story of God. If you haven't seen "The Thorn," this book will allow you to find yourself in the middle of God's epic story.

In these pages, I share stories from the pages of the Bible and from chapters of my own life. Some are adventurous, some are hilarious, and some are tragic. I hope you'll see, through this cast of characters, some threads of your own story.

As we begin this adventure together, take a few moments and consider your own story. Where are you in your life story? Are you just beginning? Somewhere in the middle? Are you close to the end, determined to finish well? Do you know how your story fits into the bigger story of God?

DAY 1

Wherever you are in life, please pray this prayer with me:

Lord, thank You for the story of my life.
Thank You for the twists and turns.
Give me eyes to see how my story fits into Your story.
Speak to my heart. Open my eyes.
Show me Your way. I'm ready.

DAY 2

THE MYSTERY OF GOD

IN THE BEGINNING ...

That's where the story of God, like all stories, starts. With a blank page, an empty space, a blinking cursor. Before anything was written or shaped or formed or created, there was a void—if you can really call it that—filled with only one thing: God.

Somehow, His presence was always here, even before there were planets and stars and trees and hummingbirds. We don't understand how that's even possible. We can't imagine how anything was always here. I mean, everything has a beginning, right?

If you bake a Texas sheet cake, you have the ingredients to start with. If you plant a garden, you have seeds. Want to make a car? Start with the raw materials. But God was just there, and then somehow the stuff of the universe was suddenly there too. But how?

The origin of the universe has baffled even the brightest minds in history. From Ptolemy to Collins to Hawking, theories of how everything came into existence are as varied as they are debated. Ultimately, we can only guess at exactly how God started it all. Beyond the imagery in Genesis chapter 1 of breath and voice and light, much about the existence of God and the beginnings of His universe remains a mystery.

The very idea of a mystery is uncomfortable and strange, yet at the same time alluring, drawing us in because it represents things that exist outside the fringes of our understanding, beyond our own imagining.

The famous movie director J. J. Abrams once gave a TED talk in which he placed a small box on a chair. The box was a child's magic kit that had the words "Mystery Box" written on it. As a boy, Abrams had asked for a magic kit for Christmas, and his parents bought him the Mystery Box, filled with surprise magic tricks.

But Abrams was so fascinated with the idea of the Mystery Box that he decided not to open it. He never did open it. During his talk, it was still wrapped in plastic. Abrams said that not knowing what was in the box made it more compelling. And that's what inspired him to tell great stories all these years. Basically, he concludes that what you don't know and what you can't see is a big part of what makes a story worth telling.

The very nature of a mystery begs questions. Who did it? Why is it there? How did it get there? What is it for? Why has it done what it's done? Will it change? How will it change? Does it matter to me? Do I matter to it?

The beginning of God's story is filled with mystery and unanswered questions. That's part of what makes it so amazing. So often, I think we try to over-explain God, especially in His beginnings. In the process, we sometimes frown on those who question or challenge or wonder about God. And then, thinking we are defending God, we declare what's in the box at the top of our lungs. But the truth is, God has designed the box so that we can never fully open it. At least not in this life.

But maybe God actually wants us to ask questions and not try to answer them all. Maybe He wants us to tumble the box around, to poke at it, to wonder what might be inside. Maybe, instead of pronouncing to the world what we are certain is in the box, we should admit we're not exactly sure ... but that we are confident that it's amazing and loving and special and important. That it really is a mystery of faith.

And then maybe, just maybe, the world around us will stop moaning about our dogma and soapboxes and begin to look at God with the sort of fascination a child has when he sees an unopened gift under the Christmas tree. And who knows? The God who somehow started it all from nothing might allow us to tear a corner off the box and get a glimpse inside.

Imagine that!

In what ways is God a mystery to you?
Remember, God doesn't get upset when we ask questions.
He loves it. It's OK to wonder, to ponder, to contemplate.
What are some of the questions you have
that you wish could be answered?

DAY 2

DAY 3

GOD MADE YOU CREATIVE

YOU ARE MORE CREATIVE THAN YOU THINK YOU ARE.

Most of us have learned to ignore our creative nature and don't believe that we're particularly creative. But the Bible says that every one of us was created in His image. And that word *image* means a lot more than looks. In fact, a better word would be *likeness*. That means that the same stuff that makes God who He is also makes us who we are. If you look around, I think you will agree that God is a pretty amazing artist. And He put that same "artisan soul," as Erwin McMannus calls it, in each of us.

The Bible tells us in Genesis chapter 1 that God created the heavens and the earth. It doesn't tell us exactly how He did it (remember, He likes mystery), and this has caused more than a little consternation and bickering and doubt ever since. We do have some hints about how He did it—His voice, His breath, mud, light, and love—but not a whole lot else.

Author Sidney Sheldon said, "A blank page is God's way of telling us how hard it is to be God."[1] As a writer, I can tell you that's the truth! If you've ever had to do a creative writing assignment and stared at a blinking cursor, you know what I'm talking about. Making something from nothing is hard.

Have you ever had one of those nights when you discover that your child has a major art project due the next morning and you're just now hearing about it? A while back, this happened with my son Chandler. He had to create a deep-sea creature out of papier-mâché. I had to run to the hobby store before it closed to buy a few bits and pieces of stuff he'd asked for. Then his mom and I sat at the kitchen table with Chandler, staring at a pile of newspaper and other crafty junk, wondering how in the world he was going to pull this off.

I watched as he worked like a mad scientist, bending coat hangers and mixing newspaper with water and flour and somehow turning the news section of the *Gazette* into a gulper eel. The thing had spines and fins and haunting eyes and glowing teeth. Honestly, it was pretty amazing. It hung from the ceiling of the art teacher's room for the remainder of the school year.

The mess on our kitchen table was overwhelming to me and my wife, but not to our son. He saw something we didn't see. The creative gift in him was able to shape and mold what others would throw away and turn it into something beautiful. That's what

---

1   Sidney Sheldon, *If Tomorrow Comes* (New York: Warner Books, 1984).

17   **DAY 3**

God does for us. That's also what God wants to do *through* us.

It's easy for us to bury or ignore the creative nudge that God wants to give us, but it's so much better to let Him work in us in ways we never expected. After all, if God can see what others can't, you can too.

He can give you ideas to reignite your marriage.

He can give you new ways to parent.

He can help you find brand-new solutions at work.

Maybe God wants to create a new business or novel or screenplay or way of helping the poor. Maybe He wants to ignite your artisan soul to develop a cure for a disease or paint a thing of beauty that points people to Him. Who's to say?

He is.

In what ways do you see the creative in your life?
In what ways do you hope that God
will show up in new and innovative ways?
Today, watch for opportunities for
God's creativity to collide with your life.
Ask Him to show you something new,
to spark ideas in you, to breathe His ingenuity
into your work, your family, and your life.

DAY 4

MADE

GOD GAVE YOU CHOICE

MY SIX-YEAR-OLD, TATE, IS A LITTLE AFRAID of the dark, so my wife and I put a few pictures on his wall that he and his siblings had painted one year at church for Easter. The paintings were all of crosses and empty tombs. We thought they'd make him feel safer.

One night, as I was lying in bed with Tate, singing him to sleep, he looked up at me and asked, "Daddy, why did Jesus have to die?"

His question surprised me. But after a moment of reflection, I answered, "Because people made some wrong choices."

A long pause. "Why did God give people choices if He knew we were going to make the wrong ones?"

I thought about that for a bit. "Because that's how God would know if we really loved Him."

To tell my son the story of God as it pertains to choices, I had to go back in time. Back to the very beginning of time.

• • •

Blank stillness. Absolute void. Nothing except for Him. Except for Love.

Then, in an instant, time began. Before this, there was no *when*, no *where*, and no space to measure. There were no physics or anything to interact with anything else. And then, suddenly, there was.

God created.

God's voice was the great catalyst.

Countless stars were born. Some leapt to life while others waxed and waned. Some exploded like cosmic fireworks, with brilliant displays of light and power. They were scattered across millions of galaxies. Billions of planets were lassoed into orbits around their suns. Pulsars warped and moaned. Black holes swallowed and shifted light like giant galactic whales, straining stars in their mouths.

God created. It's what He does. It's who He is.

Then, for reasons maybe even the angels didn't understand, His attention turned to the tiny blue speck we call Earth.

Water lulled and moved, sparkling and splashing around erupting volcanoes. Great shards of earth were pushed up and shaped. Like a potter sitting at a wheel, muddy and smiling and focused, God formed mountains and pressed out valleys. He stamped canyons and spread out sand in vast swaths.

He breathed to life the brilliant colors of the toucan and

the iridescent skin of the Man o' War. He shaped the elephant with its hilarious trunk and the giraffe with its outlandish neck and the pufferfish with its beautiful, bloated spines. The First Impressionist painted the leopard's spots and the zebra's stripes. He made the gecko's gluey feet and the hummingbird's bionic wings and the bombardier beetle's deadly potion.

Back and forth He moved across the Earth, creating, shaping, forming, carving, painting, His divine painter's coat covered in the splash of colors and alive with life.

And then He stopped. He stooped down to the rich, dark dirt He had made. His hand scooped a small amount of water from the deep. He tenderly mixed it with the dirt to make mud. For an instant, time flashed forward to another moment when God would stoop to mix dirt with water to bring sight to blind eyes (John 7:1–7). He brings life to the lifeless. It's what He does. It's who He is.

Flash back. God molds the dirt into a shape, a form. The creatures of Earth gather and gape and watch as God works. And then, God leans in further …

And breathes.

The muddy dirt comes to life. But this life is different from the stars and the clouds and the mountains and the toucans and the hummingbirds and the raccoons. There's something … familiar about this creation. Something more like God than anything else He has made.

"What is it?" the rest of creation asks.

"I have made this creation in My own image," God says. "With the ability to think, to feel, and to choose."

There it is. Choice. With choice comes the potential for sin, and with sin comes shame, and with shame comes death.

All of creation is silent, as if they know that this moment will change everything.

"Will they choose life or death?" creation asks.

"They will choose life," God says. "For a while. Then they will choose other things."

"And what will happen then?"

God sighs. He pictures another garden—one with twisted olive trees. And another figure, not unlike the one on the ground in front of Him. Since God is not bound by time or space, He knows what lies ahead. "I have a plan for that too."

That plan, of course, would be found in Jesus.

Today, as you face myriad decisions, what will you choose? Maybe yesterday you made some bad choices in the way you live or how you treat others. Every day we can start over. Today is a brand-new day.

Won't you pray this with me:

God, give me the strength to choose life today.
I reject the Enemy and his plans for me and my family.
Instead, I choose to live as I was created to live:
free and fully alive. God, today I choose You.

DAY 5

SAND

WHEN GOD GETS THE GLORY

IT'S A CRISP AUTUMN AFTERNOON, and a 240-pound running back dives over a tsunami of offensive and defensive linemen. Your living room fills with the familiar Sunday sound of cracking helmets and manly grunts. The running back goes heels over head, landing flat on his back, ball outstretched across that chalky white line. The referee's arms shoot up and the stadium explodes into chaos. Touchdown!

And then the camera zooms in as the exultant player breaks free from the pile of helmets and shoulder pads and dramatically drops his massive frame down onto one knee. He lightly kisses the middle finger and forefinger of his right hand and points triumphantly to the heavens. *God gets the glory! That one was for Him.*

But was it? Deep down, was that player really trying to reflect the glory of the Creator in that moment? Who's to say? I have to confess, moments like that tend to make me raise my eyebrows. For some reason I'm just a little bit skeptical.

The truth is, whatever the player's motives, God should get the glory whenever we use the abilities He's given us.

Let's put this into perspective. We award Best Picture honors at the Oscars to the producers of a movie, not to rolls of anamorphic film. You don't put a child's finger-painted masterpiece on your fridge to draw attention to the piece of paper covered in oils and dye. You do it to honor and celebrate its creator: the child.

You are God's masterpiece. So anything that you do that can be considered wonderful, brilliant, or noteworthy is because the Great Sculptor—the one who smoothed muscle fibers over skeletal bones—gave you the ability to do it. How could the glory not go to Him?

And yet, we so often neglect to express the praise that is rightfully due Him. And the ancient Israelites were no different. The very people the Creator chose to be His, over all other nations on the planet, spent the entirety of the Old Testament forgetting what God had done for them. Of course, God knew this would happen. So right at the beginning of the book of Exodus, He set forth a plan that so unquestionably pointed the glory back to Him, His people would reference it for thousands of years.

In Exodus chapter 1, the people of Israel were enslaved by the Egyptian empire. We don't know exactly what this slavery entailed. Cecil B. DeMille in his classic film *The Ten Commandments* would have us believe that their slavery involved a lot of brick making and mud pits, while the folks at Dreamworks in their animated tale *The Prince of Egypt* would tell you it mostly involved singing in the blistering heat. In "The Thorn," we set the scene with a couple dozen suburban Americans hauling imaginary rocks.

Regardless of the details, we know from the Scriptures that this enslavement was physically brutal and spiritually devastating. The Israelites cried out to God for deliverance for generations. Six successive lines of fathers and sons, mothers and daughters, were born into this misery and died without seeing God's answer.

At the depth of their bondage, when the entire nation was so entrenched in the system of slavery that there seemed to be no way out, God showed His might. He chose an exiled sheepherder with a debilitating speech impediment to negotiate with the most powerful ruler on Earth. And from the throat of this stutterer, God uttered the most powerful freedom cry in history: "Let my people go" (Exodus 9:1).

Then God sent a series of natural disasters that were so unbelievably supernatural, not to mention imaginative, that no earthly deliverer could take credit. Now, if I were going to send a hoard of critters to attack an oppressive civilization, I'm pretty sure I wouldn't have gone with frogs. Spiders or hornets or maniacal raccoons maybe, but frogs? That's so out of left field, only God would have thought that up. And what's more important is, it worked. As a result of these ten plagues, Pharaoh released God's people and let them go.

Then God opened up the equivalent of a six-lane highway right through the middle of a standing body of water ... and closed it as soon as His people were safe. Not even Mark Wahlberg in a '69 Camaro jumping the gap on an open ferry bridge has this kind of timing.

And that was just the beginning.

God followed up this amazing feat by creating water fountains in the middle of a desert and mysteriously air-dropping bread and quail for emergency sustenance. Not to mention a whole slew of earthquakes, fire pillars, and enough unexplainable weather to make Storm from the X-Men movies blush. Even by divine standards the exodus was a showstopper. And the Israelites praised God for it. After crossing the Red Sea, Exodus tells us of a worship session, led by Moses's sister Miriam, that was punctuated by the people's complete amazement and humility before the breathtaking power of God (Exodus 14).

The sad part is, the rest of the Old Testament includes story after story of God's people forgetting that they were His creations, chosen by Him. In every one of these seasons God sent a prophet to redirect their vision. And almost without exception, these prophets called Him "the Lord your God, who brought you out of Egypt." The way God revealed Himself in the exodus was so vivid and so clear, it provided a generations-spanning gut check for the Israelites to remember how glorious their Deliverer really was.

And now? The God who once turned billions of gallons of rushing water into blood is the same God who created the strength and agility in the NFL's MVP last Sunday. And He's the same God who enables you to do great and incredible things with the talents He has given you. Because of that, giving glory to Him isn't false humility; it's the only logical response.

I love that the people of the Old Testament added the events of Exodus to their moniker for the Creator: "the Lord your God, who brought you out of Egypt." You and I can be the kind of people who honor God like that.

What has He done for you?
What can you add to His name to remind yourself of
His power? How about:

Father God, who purged my mother of cancer
Father God, who delivered me from addiction
Father God, who breathed life into my premature baby
Father God, who … (you fill in the blank)

DAY 6

ALTARS

GOD WANTS YOU TO SEEK HIM

CHRISTIANITY DOESN'T COME WITH A MAP. Boy, it sure would be a lot easier if we could know what to expect on the road ahead. If we could anticipate roadblocks or mudslides or delays. Sometimes, when life gets busy and circumstances get tough, we wonder whether we're on the right path.

In the Old Testament, God's people built an altar whenever God did something extraordinary. They did this as a way to remember and celebrate God's faithfulness. When life got difficult, the people of God could look back at these "altars of remembrance."

Jacob built an altar to remember God's promises (Genesis 28:10–19).

Moses built an altar to remember God's victories (Exodus 17:8–16).

Joshua built an altar to remember God's protection (Joshua 4:1–8).

I live in Colorado, and I adore the outdoors. I love fishing and hiking and backpacking and just kicking around anywhere I can see the sky and smell the fresh air.

More than anything else, Colorado is best known for its mountains. They're plastered on every iconic green-and-white Colorado license plate. Lots of people move to Colorado just to be near them. Maybe to feel more "human" next to their enormous, unmovable shapes. Colorado's iconic Pike's Peak at sunset inspired Katherine Lee Bates to pen the words of "America the Beautiful."

Colorado has fifty-three "fourteeners," mountains over fourteen thousand feet tall. Some people are passionate about climbing them all. I'm not one of those people. I love to hike, but I've always hated heights. Airplanes, tall buildings, roller coasters. Not for me. But because I want people to think I'm unafraid, I do occasionally climb a mountain.

The last one I climbed was with my friend Mark. I hadn't spoken to him in nearly ten years, not since he moved to a place about thirty minutes away. But when I saw a Facebook post announcing that Christie, his wife of more than thirty years, had died, my heart sank. How hard would it have been for me to call or to hop in my truck and go see him and Christie and their two kids? I desperately wanted to find a way to make it up to him.

Two days later, when Mark posted on Facebook that he wanted to "climb a 14er," I immediately thought, *I'll go with you.* A week later, at Christie's funeral, I told him so.

"OK," he said. "How about Capital Peak next week?"

Wait, what? I didn't really want to climb a fourteener. I just wanted Mark to know that I was *willing* to do it. To show him that I knew what mattered to him. But I was caught in my own words. So I agreed to go.

After the service, I went home and looked up Capital Peak on the Internet. Was Mark insane? That mountain, according to climbing experts, is the most treacherous fourteener in Colorado!

But there was no backing out. I had to back up my boasting with my actions.

Just to get to the main path that leads to the summit, we had to hike eight miles on the Capital Peak trail. We had to go through miles of land where cattle grazed, dodging cow pies. The less-than-amazing bovine aroma overpowered the scent of wildflowers. We trudged in rain half of the time, obscuring what should have been an incredible view of the mountain we were walking toward. We groaned and smiled as our middle-aged bodies creaked and wobbled and screamed at us.

As we hiked, Mark and I talked about life, rain, cow pies, cancer, and grief. We got to know each other all over again.

After hiking till nearly sunset, we arrived at our campsite at the base of the mountain. We set up our tents, cooked a meal, and set off for bed.

As I lay in my tent, I wondered if Mark was thinking about Christie and how alone he felt and how weird it was not to have her next to him. Was he whispering to her as he lay there beneath the trees and the diamond sky? If so, what was he saying?

When I rolled over to try to get comfortable, I wondered if I would die the next day.

We woke up at five the next morning, had a quick bowl of

cold cereal, and headed up the main trail to Capital Peak. The elevation gain of the trailhead was so extreme that within five minutes, my legs started seizing up, my heart felt like it was about to burst out of my chest, and my breathing sounded like a freight train. I might as well have been hiking Everest.

We wound up the mountain trail past the tree line and up into the jagged, boulder-strewn shoulder of the mountain. As we walked, the trail grew less defined, with more rock than dirt. After a while, the trail disappeared altogether.

I looked at Mark. "How do we know which way to go?"

"Look for the cairns," he said.

A cairn is a little pile of rocks, like an altar of sorts, that someone who has taken this trail before set up as a guide, to let others know they're on track. So we followed the cairns. Walking, climbing, scrambling from one mountain altar to the next, until we reached the upper ridge of Capital.

Mark went on toward the summit, but I stopped before the infamous knife's edge. That little feature lived up to its name. Twenty-five yards of sharp rock with nothing but sheer cliff on either side of you. And the only way to cross it is to scoot on your rear. Yeah, not gonna happen.

As I sat there waiting for Mark, I again wondered what was going on in his head. Was he smiling, imagining Christy looking on and rolling her eyes at what an idiot he was? Mark told me that Christy loved it when he climbed because she knew it was in those moments that he felt closest to God. She wanted him to be near to God, living fully and free.

As dark clouds began to circle overhead, Mark scrambled back to me. We paused for a few moments atop the mountain to take in the view and to make a lame attempt to capture it on our cameras. Then we headed back down the mountain, hopping from cairn to cairn, both of us feeling a bit lighter, knowing we'd achieved our goal.

On the way back down, blue skies burst out from the gloomy clouds. The smell of wildflowers overwhelmed my senses. The view of the mountain and the valley was beyond words. The sun warmed my face and my heart.

I hiked the remaining eight miles back to the truck with a sense that something important had happened that day.

Inspired by Capital Peak, and even more by Mark, I discovered something about faith.

There have been times in my thirty-five-years-plus walk with the Lord when the trail of faith was obvious and clear and made total sense to me. And there were times when it seemed to disappear altogether. But the trail was always there, and God never left me. All I had to do was scramble to the next marker, which He left out in the open for me to see.

The cairns on that hike reminded me of those altars the people of Israel built to memorialize what God had done for them. I suspect those markers did more than that. For the broken, weary, doubting travelers who came behind, I imagine the markers served as a soul oasis.

Altars of faith provide us with proof that God exists, that He is out there, and that He wants us to find Him.

Look back on your life thus far.
Do you see a path zigzagged with little markers
of God's provision and protection and grace?
Use those memories to remind yourself that He's been
there for you, that He's with you now and He's already
been where you're headed. He wants to show you the way.

DAY 7

SILENCE

HE'S THERE EVEN IN SILENCE

A LOT HAPPENED BETWEEN THE OLD TESTAMENT and the New Testament. Historians tell us that four hundred years passed from the last words of Malachi to the first words of Matthew.

During these four hundred years, the people of Israel went from being primarily shepherds to merchants. The city of Jerusalem was sacked several times. The temple was desecrated. The priests had been bought off and the old line of Aaron was replaced with a new, more political religious class. Voices of commerce and politics and religion were everywhere, but one voice was noticeably missing.

The voice of God.

In the past, God's people were accustomed to hearing God's voice through prophets and kings and miraculous signs. Now there was cold, deafening silence. For four hundred years, it seemed that God stood like a granite statue, unspeaking, unmoving. Quietly watching and waiting.

I think I know a bit of how the people of Israel felt. Sometimes along the journey, God's voice is hard to hear and His hand is nearly invisible. He may seem silent or absent altogether.

The fall of 2008 was a difficult season for me. My family had moved from Colorado to South Carolina. A moral failure of our senior pastor had left me wounded, disillusioned, rethinking everything I had known about faith and church. I'd taken a job with an amazing church planting organization, so I was still doing work that mattered. But it wasn't the life I had imagined.

I'd always believed that God had called me to use my creative gifts to tell His story. But nothing was happening for me creatively. That year, for the first time since it began, no one was asking me to bring in "The Thorn." To make matters worse, I had just written my first novel, and my publisher asked for the advance back. Ouch. I felt like God had tuned me out and moved on.

I walked along the beach one day, picking through my doubts like shells on the seashore, feeling like my life was over and asking God where things went wrong. At one point, in desperation, I stopped, sat on the pier, and waited for Him to answer. I'm not sure what I was hoping for—maybe for God to write something in the clouds or on the water. I waited for a long time. Nothing but cold, miserable silence.

Or was it? Could it be that God was present in the silence? Perhaps He was even *more* present in the silence.

In the Old Testament (I Kings 19:11–12), God chose to reveal Himself to Elijah not in the blaze of a fire or the noise of an earthquake but in a gentle whisper. It wasn't the first time God revealed Himself that way, and it certainly wouldn't be the last. God is often more present in silence than in noise.

After forty decades of silence from God, who had spoken to His people for years through prophets, kings, and priests, the sound that broke the silence wasn't a roar or a trumpet or the clash of cymbals. God reminded us that He had been here all along through the sound of a newborn baby's cry. That day, God came near in order to complete the story of His love for us.

In the midst of the busyness of life, Jesus brings change. He makes things new. But He doesn't come to change our world. He comes to change us.

That's what God did with me in South Carolina. He did answer me. But He didn't say, "I'm going to change your life." Rather, He said, "I'm going to change *you*." Only after we submit our ideas of what should be can He make our lives what they can be. That's when life becomes "exceedingly abundantly above all that we ask or think" (Ephesians 3:20 NKJV).

Now I can look back and see the trail of His grace everywhere, even in the silence. Since that walk on the beach in 2008, I've seen tens of thousands of people find their place in God's story through "The Thorn." More than five thousand children have been rescued out of poverty through our partnership with Compassion International. Attendees have responded to the call to reach out and be the gospel to children. Creative young leaders are coming to Colorado to be trained and equipped in the arts and in culture care through The Thorn Cconservatory, a discipleship and creative leadership school with Thorn Productions.

Maybe you're going through a season of silence. Resist the temptation to turn inward. Instead, seek after God, regardless of how quiet He may seem to be. God hasn't abandoned you. And your life won't stay quiet forever. Enjoy the silence while it lasts.

Today, take a moment to just be still.
Find time to pull away from the noise of your life and
the mess of the world around you and allow God to be
present with you in the silence. For a few minutes, turn
off the music, put away your cell phone, and sit with God.
Remember all the good things He has done for you.

DAY 8

TRUST

TRUSTING GOD WHEN
YOU DON'T UNDERSTAND

AS THE PRODUCER OF A LIVE STAGE SHOW, I've learned that things don't always go as planned. Over the past twenty years, we've had Jesus fall off the cross, an audience member punch Satan in the face, a guardian angel light his hair on fire, a disciple fall through a hole in the stage, the tomb catch on fire, and a remote-control platform drive itself right off the stage. We've had music tracks not work, lighting boards crash, technicians hit the wrong cue, and props and sets fall down. You name it, it's probably happened.

We've gotten used to improvising. It's live theater, so it's what we do. But in life, it's not always easy to adjust when things don't go as planned. Life isn't predictable. Cars break down. Flights are missed. Companies downsize. People fall ill. Life is full of "I didn't see that coming" moments. The Bible is full of those moments too.

I'm guessing that Jesus' stepfather, Joseph, was a man who cut once and measured twice. The sort of guy who believed things when he saw them. He probably didn't get too excited about the latest fad or the newest gadget. As a craftsman, he preferred doing things the old-fashioned way, like they'd always been done, like his father before him had done them.

As a carpenter, I imagine that Joseph spent hundreds of hours, maybe thousands, with his father in the workshop. I can almost see him, bending over a lathe in the late afternoon, with the sun streaking through the dust in the shop, leveling out a board until it was perfectly straight.

He'd learned how to cut and measure and form. He understood the importance of careful instruction and precise execution. He knew the value of strong wood, tight bolts, and joints that didn't wobble. He knew what it took to build a table or chair or bed. He knew they didn't just build themselves. First the idea, then a plan, then the work. No surprises.

I wonder how Joseph felt when Mary told him that she was pregnant with the Son of God. For a man who was used to careful plans, it must have come as quite a shock.

"But Mary, I don't understand. How—"

"Joseph, I'm telling you, it was God. An angel came to me."

Imagine the thoughts that must have been swirling in Joseph's head. Doubt would have come crashing through like a hurricane making landfall. The crushing pain of betrayal, albeit unfounded, must have surrounded him, threatening to choke the life from his heart.

Joseph couldn't believe what Mary told him. Maybe he wanted to, but he just couldn't. The pain was too much. The feelings of rejection were too strong. He began writing up the divorce papers in his head. What would he give as the reason? Adultery. The sting was more than Joseph could bear.

I suspect that once he got back to the wood shop, Joseph probably had a hard time hiding his feelings.

"What's wrong, Son?" his father asks.

Joseph shakes his head as if everything's OK.

But after his father leaves the workshop, hot tears burn down Joseph's face. He works the lathe with passion, a combination of anger and ache releasing with every stroke. Unanswered questions. Vivid imaginations. Unfounded accusations.

At the end of the day, after all the pain and questions and doubts, Joseph finally falls asleep. And there, in a dream, an angel of God visits him.

She's telling the truth.

You will have a son.

It will be God's.

His name will be Jesus.

He will save the people from their sins.

Did Joseph see anything as the angel spoke? Did he envision flashes of wood, beams crisscrossed on a lonely hillside? Nails being driven into flesh? Perhaps. We don't know.

When the dream is over, Joseph sits up with a jolt. *It's all true!*

Joseph goes to Mary, full of grace and forgiveness and love. She's going to have a baby. God's Son. And Joseph will adopt Him.

Fast-forward thirty years.

Joseph walks into the workshop. Jesus has been there since sunrise. He is working hard, hand pressed down on a lathe, sweat dripping from His face. Or are those tears?

"What's wrong, Son?"

Jesus shakes his head as if everything's OK.

Joseph leaves the workshop with tears streaming down his face. But this time, it's not because of rejection or fear or anger. These are tears of thankfulness and joy … and maybe a little sadness. He knows it's time. He can sense it. He thanks the Father for the thirty years he had with Jesus.

That's how it goes with us too. There are moments in life when everything we know comes into question. Times when we feel abandoned, alone, afraid. Hot tears streak across cheeks wrinkled with pain. We ask how and why.

In those moments, God wants to visit us. He sees us and understands us, and He has a plan bigger than we know. In those moments, He asks us to set aside our own plans and adopt His plans, His course, His assignment for our lives.

Today, why not say yes?

Read Matthew 1:18–24. Consider what it must have been like for Joseph to handle the news of Mary being pregnant with Jesus. Now consider whatever situation you're facing that seems difficult or frightening or overwhelming. Determine to trust in God like Joseph did.

We don't know what the future holds. But God does. And He's faithful. He will walk with us. We need only to put our trust in Him and take His hand.

DAY 9

BARN

GOD SEES WHAT YOU DON'T SEE

THE INNKEEPER TOSSED AND TURNED IN HIS SLEEP all night. In his dreams he saw the face of a traveler from Nazareth. Weariness mixed with fear in the young man's eyes. When the face of his dreams appeared at his door the next day, the innkeeper wasn't completely surprised.

"Is there any room?" the young traveler asked, peering into the inn.

The innkeeper shook his head. He had already turned away others, and he'd been scowled and cussed at. Crowds seemed to bring out the worst in people. He started to close the door, but

41

a hand stopped him.

"Please. My wife is pregnant."

A woman appeared in the shadows behind the young man. She was sitting on a donkey, bent over and groaning.

"The baby could come tonight."

There really was no room. Not just here, but anywhere. With a sigh, he offered them the stable. It was all that he could do.

Or was it?

When he told his wife about the visitors, she scolded him for not offering more. After all, a stable is no place for a baby to be born. He could have offered the young couple a place in their own home. Even their own bed.

We don't know exactly how Jesus' birthplace looked. It could have been a cave, a barn, or a corral. But we do know it wasn't a gilded throne. No, the Son of God was born in a manger lined with straw. Instead of royal attendants, bleary-eyed shepherds came by to bear witness to His majesty. Where trumpets and drums would have announced a royal birth, the bleating of sheep and the thumping of hoofs were the heralding sounds of His arrival.

I would have done things differently. I might have announced His arrival with something like a Super Bowl halftime show or a Washington DC Fourth of July celebration. I would definitely have included fireworks and special effects and the latest in technology to really ramp it up.

As the producer of "The Thorn," I love finding ways to punctuate the big moments. If I can use neon lights or fog or pyrotechnics, I usually say, "Go for it." But that's not how God works.

We might have chosen for the Messiah to be born of a royal family or maybe a movie star. No one suspected the Son of God would come into this world through the womb of a teenager from Nowheresville. We would have planned for Him to get His training at an Ivy League university, not in a woodworker's shop. No one would have imagined that the Majesty of Heaven would be born in a lonely barn and die on a craggy hillside.

But that's just like God. He loves to work in ways that we would never expect. And following Him is rarely clean and tidy. Faith is messy and unpredictable because God works in ways we wouldn't expect.

And God sees what we don't see.

We might see a business on the brink of bankruptcy and God sees an opportunity for hope. We see a family in crisis and He sees a way for grace to invade our everyday lives. We see a person broken and lonely, but God sees a son or daughter He loves more than you could ever imagine. When things look bleak or hopeless, God sees what we don't see.

At one point during the Last Supper, Jesus knelt down to wash His disciples' feet. Peter was taken aback, but Jesus said to him, "You don't understand now what I am doing, but someday you will" (John 13:7 NLT). That's the same thing Jesus says to us when we don't understand what He seems to be up to in our lives.

Turn to Him today. Run into His arms.
Ask Him to give you His eyes for your family,
your husband, your children, your home, your business,
your city. Where we see ruin, He sees redemption.
Where we see failure, He sees a bright future.
We may not understand it now, but someday we will.

DAY 10

LOST

WHEN FEAR BEARS DOWN

A FEW YEARS AGO, I BROUGHT MY TWO OLDEST BOYS on a trip to Europe as the final step in a coming-of-age journey we invented called the Bolin Quest. Our adventures took us from the Eiffel Tower to the Roman Coliseum to Buckingham Palace.

One day, as I stood on the edge of the River Thames, I gazed up at the House of Parliament, with its beautiful windows and spires. I saw Westminster Abbey, with its grand gothic arches. I could see Big Ben, the quintessential icon of London. But I didn't see my boys.

The sun was beginning to set as I stood there in the shadow of the London Eye, desperately scanning the throngs of people for my two newly minted teenagers. My worst fears twisted their way around my heart—the boys weren't late, they were missing. What began as a special family trip to Europe had become a nightmare.

I paced the riverbank, trying to convince myself that there was a logical explanation for their absence. But I couldn't find it. More than an hour earlier, we had left Westminster Abbey, planning to cross the bridge and catch a ride on Europe's highest Ferris wheel. The boys, excited about being in London on an adventure with Dad, asked me if they could ride the Tube by themselves instead of walking with me. It seemed like a great way for them to flex their new muscles of independence.

After the boys descended into the bowels of the London Underground, I realized we hadn't made any plans for what to do if they got lost. We couldn't call each other because, when we'd arrived a few days earlier, I told them to turn off their phones so they wouldn't incur any crazy-high international charges. I hadn't thought to tell them that it was OK to turn on their phones if they became lost in a city of ten million people. Good move, Dad.

Over an hour later, I finally caved and called my wife in Colorado.

"Uh, hi, babe."

"Hi, hon. How are you and the boys? Having fun?"

I gulped. "Well … now, don't freak out, but I need your help. Can you do a 'find your friends' on your iPhone?"

After a short pause, she asked, "Why?"

"Um, I don't actually know where the boys are this exact minute."

"What do you mean?"

"They may or may not be somewhere in the London subway system."

"You let the boys go off alone in Europe?" You can probably imagine some of the other things Sarah said at that point.

After we hung up, Sarah tried to find them. With no luck.

My stomach was churning. My eyes were getting blurry. I knew I was in serious trouble.

"Have you prayed?" Sarah asked when she called me back.

In the rush of everything, I hadn't. We prayed together. Before we even said amen, I saw the boys, walking up a path along the river, munching on roasted peanuts and laughing.

I ran to them. "Are you OK?"

Chandler glanced at Harrison, who looked a bit more shaken up than his older brother. "We missed our stop, so we got off a few stops later. We could see the Ferris wheel, so we decided to walk to it."

Harrison grinned. "I told Chandler, 'Dad loves adventure. He'll think it's great that we're doing this.'"

I did love adventure. I had taught my boys to embrace risk and new experiences, but also to use wisdom. They had done exactly that. In that moment, they had taken a big step toward becoming men. And I had taken a big step in understanding that more often than not, our fears are unfounded.

Mary and Joseph must have had a similar experience when Jesus was twelve years old (Luke 2:41–52). Every year, they made the five-day journey from Nazareth to Jerusalem with their friends and relatives. But this time, when everyone else headed home, Jesus stayed back in Jerusalem, unbeknownst to his parents.

That night, as the sun began to set, Joseph secured the camp, tucked in the kids, and blew out the oil lamps. But when Joseph counted heads he came up one short.

Joseph walks back to the main tent to find Mary. "Uh, sweetheart, it looks like … How do I say this?"

"Just say it, Joseph."

"Jesus seems to be missing."

Just imagine what must have gone through Mary's mind. They had misplaced the Savior of the world!

Mary flips back tent doors and rushes to her relatives' camps, all the while calling for Jesus like a panic-stricken parent at Disney World.

She searches everywhere, but no Jesus. Joseph suggests that maybe He stayed back in Jerusalem for some reason. Mary or Joseph might have had relatives there, but probably not. The feast of Passover drew tens of thousands to Jerusalem, so the city was filled with people—good and bad alike.

As Mary and Joseph ride back to Jerusalem, frightening thoughts go through their heads. Where is Jesus? Is He safe? Is He in trouble? If you've ever lost your kids, even for a few minutes, you know the fear that must have gripped their hearts.

When they get back to Jerusalem, they don't find Jesus waiting for them at the city gates. They spend three days searching, running, crying, begging for answers, with moist eyes and churning stomachs. Finally, they find Jesus in the temple, teaching.

Mary runs to Jesus, pulling Him into an embrace. Joseph breathes a deep sigh of relief.

Jesus says, "Where did you expect to find Me? I was in My Father's house." He said it with respect—much like my son said to me, "We knew you'd love it if we had some adventure." Jesus was saying, "You know Me better than anyone in the world. I assumed that you would know I was here, doing what I was born to do."

How did Mary respond after everything calmed down? Did

she get mad at God? Or at Joseph for not watching closer? Did she scold Jesus? No. Scripture says that she "treasured up all these things in her heart" (Luke 2:51 ESV).

How do you respond when things seem out of control?
Do you panic and blame God?
Do you allow your faith in your fears
to be bigger than your faith in God?
Or do you trust that God is at work behind
the scenes, maybe just out of view?
In what ways can you give your worries to
God and begin to trust Him more deeply today?

DAY 11

SAWDUST

STEP OUT OF THE ORDINARY

SOMETHING MYSTERIOUS AND powerful happens when we make the choice to step away from the ordinary world.

In 1492, Columbus left the land of his birth to set sail across the ocean, and history would mark the day. Frodo Baggins left the comfort of the Shire to begin an adventure that would forever change him and alter the destiny of Middle Earth. King David left a simple life as a shepherd in exchange for a king's scepter. Jesus left the ordinariness of His father's wood shop to embark on what would be the greatest adventure of all time.

Before Columbus became a cross-Atlantic explorer, he was a middle-class wool weaver. Before Frodo became the lynchpin in the epic story of The Lord of the Rings, he was basically a sit-at-home trust-fund baby. Before the king of Israel became "David the Giant Slayer," he was just David the sheepherder. Before Jesus changed the molecular structure of water into a vintage merlot, before He repaired the optic nerves of a blind man or began raising people from the dead, He was building shelves and sanding tables.

Now, there's nothing wrong with "ordinary." It's safe and secure and comforting. The everyday world is full of routine and habits that make us feel grounded. Those things are beautiful and simple.

But then something happens to break the routine. Usually it comes as a surprise.

One day, as Columbus was weaving wool, his brother-in-law showed him a map that showed the world as a sphere, not flat. In that moment, Columbus realized he could sail the world. When his beloved wife, Filipa, died, he and his son Diego moved to Spain, from which he would eventually sail the ocean blue.

Frodo was busy in his garden when he was visited by a mysterious old friend, Gandalf. In the quiet of Frodo's hobbit hole, Gandalf told him of the adventures that lay ahead. Frodo quipped back to Gandalf that they didn't want any adventures. If you've read the book or seen the movie, you know how that turned out. The next scene shows Frodo leaving the Shire for the first time in his life, heading toward the Inn of the Prancing Pony.

In the silence of an open field, David worshipped God while he watched his father's sheep, keeping a wary eye for anything that could harm them. When he left his sheep to obey his father's request to visit his brothers on the front lines of battle, David's life changed. He may not have seen it coming, but killing Goliath with nothing more than a stone and a sling would redirect the course of not only his life, but the history of Israel.

And even though Jesus had been the Cocreator of the universe, before He began His journey that would change the world, the one who had once split atoms was busy splitting wood for His earthly father, Joseph. Like Columbus and Frodo, Jesus chose to answer the call to leave His ordinary world in order to rescue it. Unlike Columbus or Frodo, Jesus knew what was ahead of Him, what He would endure, and ultimately, how the story would end.

Jesus has a way of invading our ordinary world and calling us to something we never expected. He finds us in the carpool lane, typing away in a cubicle, working on a construction site, or sitting in class. And, like Gandalf, He invites us to embark on an adventure that could change our lives.

Maybe the adventure doesn't involve dragons or dwarves or treasure. And maybe it doesn't mean changing your job or moving overseas. Perhaps the adventure He's calling you on is praying like never before or serving in a way you've never imagined. God's calling is not always a *bigger* or *better* thing. But it almost always involves leaving something behind. Old habits. Entrenched ideas. Life as we know it.

He doesn't just call us out of the ordinary and into His adventure once. He does it over and over, as long as we allow Him to.

Today, Jesus is calling you to step out of the ordinary world and into His adventure for you. Yes, there will still be dishes and laundry and final exams, but even those things will hold different meaning for us when we accept the call.

Stepping out of the ordinary world doesn't necessarily change the things around us; it changes us. For Jesus, the ordinary life

He led growing up prepared Him for His extraordinary ministry. But when the time came, He willingly hung up His carpenter's apron and took on the rabbi's robe. Stepping out of the carpentry shop and onto the roads of Nazareth started an adventure that would shake the world.

Jesus is calling us out of monotony and into His adventure. Truly, He has come so that we may have life "and have it abundantly" (John 10:10 ESV).

God wants to call you out of your comfort zone. Will you accept the call? Maybe He is calling you to reach out to someone even though you're not an outgoing person ... or to be truly vulnerable for the first time in your life ... or to register for a class or sign up to lead a small group. In what ways can you step out of your comfort zone and into God's adventure for you?

DAY 12

WHISPER

GOD WANTS TO GET YOUR ATTENTION

GOD OFTEN USES SILENCE TO GET OUR ATTENTION. But not always. Sometimes He chooses the most unexpected things to turn our eyes and hearts toward Him.

Out in the wilderness, God used a dove hovering over Jesus as a way to get the attention of John the Baptist. In a nearby wilderness a few hundred years earlier, God used a burning bush to get the attention of Moses. But that's not even close to the end of the list. God loves to invade our normal lives in hopes of invading our hearts.

If you're Abraham and your ninety-year-old wife gets pregnant, you tend to pay attention.

If you're Elijah and God sends birds to feed you, you take notice.

If you're Saul and Jesus appears to you on the road to Damascus, you listen to what He has to say.

And God didn't stop working this way. In fact, history is full of stories of Him getting people's attention in startling ways.

In 1942, God used a seagull to get the attention of James Whittaker, who was adrift at sea with the famous pilot Eddie Rickenbacker.

In 1738, John Wesley unwillingly attended a small group and found his "heart strangely warmed."

Augustine sat in a garden, debating between visiting his mistress or reading his Bible, which lay open nearby. When he heard a voice saying, "Pick it up, pick it up," he did.

Read the stories of C. S. Lewis, Bob Dylan, or Francis Collins, and you'll see that the Hound of Heaven will do whatever it takes to get someone's attention.

Anne Lamott describes her moment of conversion beautifully yet simply.

While lying in bed one night, she felt a presence with her in her room, "hunkered down in the corner." Though she did not see anyone there, she knew it was Jesus.

"I thought about my life and my brilliant, hilarious, progressive friends, I thought about what everyone would think of me if I became a Christian, and it seemed an utterly impossible thing that simply could not be allowed to happen. I turned to the wall and said out loud, 'I would rather die.'"

When she awoke in the morning, the presence was gone, but she had the feeling of being followed around by a cat wherever she went. She knew that if she fed the "cat" or let it in, it would stay forever. So Anne tried to keep ahead of the cat at all times. Yet it kept pursuing her.

A week later, Anne went to church so hung over that she could barely stand. But she was so taken by the final worship song that she opened herself to the feeling and allowed it to wash over her. She left before the benediction and raced home, with the cat trailing behind her. When she got to her house, she took a long, deep breath and said out loud, "I quit. All right. You can come in."[2]

I love how The Message describes God's love in Psalm 23:6. "Your beauty and love chase after me every day of my life." God used a dove, a burning bush, a neighbor's voice, and an imaginary cat to bring people to Him. In my own life, God has used strangers, crazy-tight finances, and even my dog, Trooper, to get my attention. I wonder what He'll use in your life.

---

2   Anne Lamott, *Traveling Mercies* (Anchor Books, 2000).

DAY 13

FOLLOW

JESUS IS CALLING YOU

HAVE YOU EVER IMAGINED what it must have been like to be one of the people Jesus chose to follow Him? There were a lot of folks walking around Galilee when Jesus picked His team. Why did He select those twelve? You know, it's one thing to get picked in junior high to be on the dodgeball team with the cool kids, but it's entirely another thing to be one of the dozen people on the planet chosen by the one who created the grains of dust in the baseball diamond and who breathed life into the grass of the soccer field.

If I had been alive two thousand years ago and happened to walk by Jesus on the day He called His first disciples, would He have stopped me and asked me to follow Him? On some days, I think He would have. On most days, I don't.

About fifteen years ago, I was in Israel, and I stayed in a little hotel near the Sea of Galilee. It wasn't fancy, just a modest little inn where weary travelers could spend the night near the lapping waters of the sea.

There were gardens in the back of the hotel and a little path that led down to the water. Palm trees swayed in the breeze that lifted off the sea and cooled the edges of the hot desert around it.

Prior to that trip, I had been dealing with a ball of emotions and personal conflict. My wife was pregnant with our first child. That was a big deal because we'd been trying to have children for five years. Sarah was almost nine months pregnant, ready to give birth at any time, when I left for Israel.

I'd also just lost a dream business after someone I trusted embezzled more than this small company could bear. The crushing loss of my little outdoor store and the gut-wrenching bankruptcy had been devastating and humiliating.

At the time, I was leading a vibrant youth ministry. On the outside, I seemed happy, but on the inside I was a wreck. I needed Jesus more than ever.

That night in the hotel by the sea, I couldn't sleep. At midnight, I got up, slipped into my sandals, and went down to the beach. I walked along the shoreline, praying for my wife and our unborn baby and for my dying dreams.

Suddenly, the scenery around me faded. In its place, I could envision people from Jesus' time walking along the beach. I saw women with their children, who were running and laughing and skipping rocks in the water. I saw an old man with a long white beard, praying as he walked. I saw fishermen in boats, working their nets.

DAY 13

And then I saw Him.

At first I wanted to run back to my hotel room and crawl under the sheets. But I couldn't move.

He walked straight toward me, His hands stretched out to me. He was focused on me, like I was all that mattered to Him. He stepped right up to me and said, "Follow Me."

I fell to my knees and wept. Jesus loved me, just as I was, conflicted and narcissistic and hurt and ambitious. He was willing to take it all. He wanted to make something beautiful out of my life, and I wanted that more than anything else in the world.

That same Jesus is walking toward you today, with His arm stretched out. Whether you're a mom who struggles to make it through carpool without bursting into tears from the stress of raising kids on your own. Or a dad parked alone on a street with your head on the steering wheel because you have no idea how you're going to dig your family out of the financial hole you're in. Whether you're the black sheep or the prodigal son or the perfect kid, Jesus is there for you. He's looking for you. He's waiting for you. He wants more than anything to turn your life into something beautiful for Him. He wants to invite you into His story.

If you've ever wondered whether Jesus would invite you to follow Him, I have good news. He already has. All you have to do is accept His invitation.

How can you answer Jesus' call and begin to walk more closely with Him today? Maybe just by setting aside a few minutes to be with Him. Or giving up something in your life that takes time and attention away from Jesus and the things in life that matter most.

Would you pray this with me right now:

Jesus, today I am deciding to follow You.
I'm determined to be Your follower.
I accept Your call on my life and surrender
fully to You all over again today.

• • •

Jesus said to His disciples,
"Whoever wants to be my disciple
must deny themselves and take up
their cross and follow me."

(Matthew 16:24).

• • •

DAY 14

FISH

GOD MADE YOU FOR A PURPOSE

SEVERAL YEARS AGO, MY SON CHANDLER CONVINCED MY WIFE AND ME to get a new family dog—more specifically, his own dog. Trooper is a white English cream golden retriever. A few months after we brought him home to live with us, I casually told my wife that we should have him professionally trained.

"What?" Sarah scowled.

"You know, for obedience ... and bird hunting."

She rolled her eyes. "You do know that you have *never* been bird hunting, right?"

It's true. I grew up in Nebraska, and I've gone hunting for small game, but not for birds. I've always imagined what it would be like to get up early, put on my camo jacket, pour a steaming cup of coffee, and sit in a duck blind until the sun hit the river just perfectly. I'd see the ducks, take out three or four in one shot, and then my dog would dash from the blind and bring them back. Every moment of the experience would be worthy of the cover of *Sports Illustrated*.

"Uh, hello?" Sarah said, snapping me back to reality.

"Yeah, yeah," I said. "We'll see."

For the next few weeks, I kept telling Sarah we needed to have Trooper trained for obedience … and bird hunting. She kept telling me I was crazy. I'd sulk. Then Trooper would jump on someone or dig a hole in the yard the size of China or do exactly the opposite of whatever we wanted him to do. There was no question—that dog needed to be trained.

When Sarah finally gave in, I looked for the best hunting school I could find. After I got Trooper signed up, my son and I jumped into my truck and dropped him off at Hideaway Kennels for a doggy equivalent to an education at West Point. Three months and a lot of money later, we picked up our pet. His transformation was amazing. The new Trooper obeyed on command and did whatever we told him to do. He could even flush and retrieve birds!

That was three years ago and Trooper has yet to go hunting. Trust me, I had every intention of taking him. But I never did. He became an incredible hunting dog, yet I never used him to the fullest extent of his purpose.

Many of us are like my dog. God has put all this remarkable potential in us, but we're still wandering around wondering what we're supposed to be doing.

When Jesus called Peter and Andrew, He said, "Follow me ... and I will send you out to fish for people" (Matthew 4:19).

Now, these guys understood what it meant to fish. They were used to early mornings and patience over long stretches of no action. They knew the importance of the right bait and the right spot. They were well trained as fishermen.

But Jesus said that if they followed Him, He would give them a whole new purpose. Notice that He didn't say, "Follow Me and I'll make you rich," or, "Follow Me and I'll make you happy." He said, "Follow Me and I'll send you out to fish for people."

Our purpose is to follow Jesus. As we do, He will leverage our passions and talents to advance His kingdom. After all, He designed us with those passions and talents.

Some of us love numbers and others love art. Some people love process and strategy and others work best in the midst of chaos. God sees the big picture and designs the mosaic of His church with people as diverse as you can imagine. Wonder what God's assignment for you is? Your talents and passions are good clues.

Peter was a fisherman. Jesus made him a fisher of people.

Paul was a statesman. He became the main apologist of the early church.

Luke was a physician. He was assigned to be the surgical scribe of the gospel.

Nicodemus was a theologian. God turned him into a bridge builder to the religious.

Just like my pup already has it in him to be a great hunting dog, we've already got within us the raw material that God wants to use. Our deepest purpose is to love Him and to make Him known. How do we do that? We follow Him and allow Him to use the things that He has already placed in us.

Spend a few moments alone with God and a piece of paper and make a list of the things you do well, the tasks you excel at. Then make a list of the things you're passionate about. Consider ways that those two lists might combine. Chances are, there's a place at the intersection of your talents and your interests that God wants to use to equip you to draw others to Him and proclaim His kingdom.

• • •

"For I know the plans I have for you," declares the Lord, "plans to prosper you and not to harm you, plans to give you hope and a future."

(Jeremiah 29:11)

• • •

DAY 14

DAY 15

ORDINARY

JESUS IS LOOKING FOR ORDINARY PEOPLE

I'M WRITING THIS IN THE FALL, and I just told my wife that we should decorate for the holidays.

Now, Sarah and I are not good decorators. We have friends who have "the gift." Going over to their house is like walking into a Pinterest page. Our style looks like a Hobby Lobby crashed into an IKEA.

But Sarah and I have other things we do really well. My wife can out-cook anyone I know. And as a guy who loves a good risotto, cooking ranks about fourteen notches above Pinterest on my personal scale of awesomeness.

To be honest, when I look at Pinterest or Facebook or Instagram, I wonder where these people find the time to paint, carve, arrange, and put together decor for every imaginable holiday and season. I'm lucky if I get around to sticking a few soggy pumpkins on our front porch before the little door knockers come calling.

Some people seem desperate for their lives to be perceived as exceptional and extraordinary—at least to their many social media fans. Have you ever spent thirty minutes typing a two-sentence status update, rewriting each word to paint yourself as insightful and wise yet whimsical? Have you tried out every single Instagram filter to perfectly represent the "reality" of your totally everyday encounter with something beautiful? Or worked hard to find just the right angle of a picture that says, "Look how unbelievably breathtaking my totally ordinary life is"?

I'm not saying you're bragging. I'm sure your life really is amazing. From sunsets that bake the evening sky into a canvas of glowing autumn colors to the perfectly grilled bacon-wrapped fillet you're having for dinner, nestled between asparagus as green as grass and mashed potatoes fluffier than Pixar clouds—all grown in your own garden, of course. Why not post about it?

But these snapshots do not represent your everyday life.

Could you imagine what it would be like if the Facebook you were the real you? Everything around you would be unbelievably adorable. Your teenagers would always be winning at sports or going to the prom or getting their driver's licenses. Your marriage would be incredible because all of the amazing things you say about your spouse on your anniversary are true the other 364 days of the year as well. All you would ever do is go to big-league football games, once-in-a-lifetime concerts, and exotic vacation locations.

If only.

For most of us, the lives we live on social media are different from the lives we live every day. The kids are irritating more often than they're adorable. Our teenagers require us to negotiate peace pacts with the skill of a Middle Eastern ambassador. Instead of serving up five-star dinners with china and silverware and crystal goblets so pristine they would make Gordon Ramsay blush, we're reheating leftovers on paper plates.

On Facebook, everyone is writing a best seller or taking a vacation or celebrating another amazing anniversary. In real life, we struggle to finish the book we're reading, not to mention the one we're writing. If we manage to take a break from carpool, laundry, and picking up dog poop to go on a vacation or celebrate a special occasion, the event often doesn't live up to our expectations ... and then we're back to our ordinary lives.

That's what so great about Jesus. He was the extraordinary wrapped in the ordinary. And He picked ordinary people to surround Himself with during His ministry. If I had been Jesus, and I were putting together my "dream team," it probably wouldn't have included an IRS worker, a mobster, a paid assassin, and a few guys who looked like they walked off the TV show *The Deadliest Catch.*

I would have made sure my team included a financial wizard, a few professional athletes, maybe a celebrity or two, a politician, and an off-the-charts amazing administrator. But if I allow this to become my impression of the team that Jesus wants, it colors the way I see myself. Then I have to strive to be one of the few who can make the cut.

I think, *If I can become a best-selling author, then Jesus can use my talents to reach people. He could really use me if my book gets turned into a movie that's shown in theaters. Then people all over America can see it.*

As if my ordinary world isn't good enough for Jesus to use.

The opposite perspective has the same results. Have you ever been in a group of believers who are all telling their testimonies, and you're desperately scrolling through the history of your life trying to find the extraordinary moment of darkness that will show how far God has brought you? You find yourself wishing you'd been a drug addict in high school. Or that you had to fight that eating disorder a little longer. Anything to make Christ's victory in your life seem more impressive. And to make your life appear less ordinary.

But that's not how Jesus works. He isn't always looking for the most dramatic success story. He's just looking for you.

About ten years after Jesus went back to heaven, the church was growing and the twelve apostles needed help taking care of the widows. One of the twelve, Stephen, stepped up and agreed to become a food pantry attendant. Not a conference speaker or best-selling author. Just a servant.

Stephen collected food from those who had it and passed it out to those who didn't. Was he in charge of food donations all across the Roman Empire? Nope. Just for the Greeks in his community. And he was one out of six guys doing it.

But eventually Stephen was promoted and became the most innovative charity worker of his day, right? Nope. He died serving food to the widows in his city.

Today we remember Stephen for being the first martyr in church history. But I'm not sure that is what pleased his Father the most. When he met Jesus moments after his death, I imagine Jesus looked at him and said, "Thank you for feeding My daughters. Thank you for serving the ones I gave you."

Let's not pretend to be who we're not. And let's not wait for the big moments in life to serve God. Let's start today. Remember,

God isn't looking for extraordinary people. He's looking for the ones who are willing to serve Him.

Pray this with me:

God, use me today however You want to.
I surrender myself, my ego, and my expectations to You.
Show me how to serve You by serving
those around me who need You the most.
I want my life to be less about me and more about You.

• • •

He said to me, "My grace is sufficient for you, for my power is made perfect in weakness." Therefore I will boast all the more gladly about my weaknesses, so that Christ's power may rest on me.

(2 Corinthians 12:9)

• • •

DAY 16

EVERYDAY

GOD INVADES OUR MUNDANE MOMENTS

THE BIBLE IS FULL OF UNANSWERED QUESTIONS.

After the flood, did Jonah ever eat fish again?

After the burning bush incident, did Moses avoid shrubbery?

After the resurrection, did Pilate start listening to his wife?

Did Mary ever ask James if he could be more like his older brother?

We don't know. We can only guess at the stories that lie within the margins and between the verses of the Bible. But oh, we can imagine.

At every showing of "The Thorn," the cast and crew offer a behind-the-scenes tour, where select people get to see what the rest of the audience never does. How does Jesus get from the cross to the tomb so quickly? How do the angels fly? How do we do the makeup on the demons? Those who look behind the scenes get an entirely different view of the show.

I think if we could look behind the scenes in the Bible, we'd get a totally different perspective on them too.

For example, I've often wondered what was going on during Jesus' first miracle, the wedding in Cana (John 2:1–11). We know that a couple was getting married. Someone would have been in charge of the wedding feast. Usually that job went to a man, but let's imagine it was a woman. We'll call her Rebecca. Maybe she was sort of like a maid of honor. Her job was to make sure everything was perfect for the bride, her best friend since childhood.

Rebecca is determined to make this the most perfect wedding feast of all time. After all, her best friend is finally getting married to the man of her dreams. Rebecca and her husband work painstakingly to make sure everything is in order. Everyone has been invited, and since Cana is a small town, Rebecca expects a big crowd.

On the day of the feast, the food has been prepared, the wine poured, and the tables set. Rebecca has placed flowers everywhere, so the aroma of chamomile and lavender fill the area.

As the sun is just about to set, the feast begins. Rebecca watches tearfully as the new couple walks in. The bride looks radiant, beaming with new love. Everyone cheers and sing. Food is served and the celebration begins.

For the next several hours, everyone laughs and dances and eats and drinks. Then Rebecca's mother tugs on her sleeve, a desperate look on her face.

"What is it, Mom?"

"The wine is running out."

Rebecca's heart sinks. She has done everything she could to prepare for this important event. How could she have forgotten to order enough wine? Frantic, she looks around the courtyard but finds nothing. She asks a few friends, but no one has enough extra wine for the wedding. Tears well up in her eyes with the realization that she needs to tell her best friend about her mistake.

As she walks toward the bride and groom, she passes by a group of guests who have come up from Nazareth. One of them asks her what's wrong. She tells them. One of the guests—a man she's been told is named Jesus—gazes at her with eyes that seem to look right into her soul. All at once, her anxiety goes away. She takes a deep breath and sits down.

Then she watches as Jesus walks over to the clay pots that are usually used for water. He stands there for a moment, as if He's praying. Then he tells the servants to serve the wedding guests.

When the men pour from the clay pots into the guests' drinking glasses, Rebecca notices it's not water anymore but wine! And not just everyday wine. Jesus has turned the water into the best wine she has ever tasted.

The wedding feast goes on. As the bride and groom thank their guests and the people go back to their homes, Rebecca stands alone in the courtyard, thinking about how God used Jesus to take care of the one thing that mattered the most to her.

Of course, we don't really know what was happening behind the scenes in this story. But I can assure you there was someone getting nervous about the wine. And for reasons we don't really understand, Jesus chose to use this moment as the first miracle of His ministry. Most theologians point to this wedding feast as the start of His three years of ministry.

If it were me, I would have chosen a more dramatic miracle as my opening act. Maybe parting the Sea of Galilee or calling down fire from heaven. Jesus could have started out by feeding twenty thousand people with a few loaves of bread. Or walked on water or raised someone from the dead. But He didn't. Instead, He chose to perform a miracle that in the end would only really matter to a few people, people who mattered to Him.

The daughter of a close friend of mine planned for a beautiful outdoor wedding in Colorado. But the weather didn't cooperate. Storm clouds rolled in and the temperature dropped. The setting was beautiful, with white chairs and a big white tent. But the attendees were huddled together under a nearby shelter, trying to stay warm.

While the wedding party assured the bride and groom that everything was going to be OK, a friend of the family named Gary went off to one of his job sites and picked up several high-powered construction heaters. Before any of us knew what was happening, Gary had quietly set up the heaters.

Within a few minutes, everyone was warm and smiling and dancing. The reception went on for hours, and it was one of the most fun and memorable events I've ever attended. All because one person decided to make what mattered to someone else matter to him.

Have you ever wanted to pray about something but didn't because it seemed too petty or small or insignificant to bother God with? I mean, isn't He busy with the really important things, like world hunger and global warming and cancer?

If it matters to you, it matters to God.

And if it matters to God, it should matter to us. When we go out of our way to help someone, we're being Jesus to that person.

---

*In what small way can you glorify God
in the middle of your ordinariness?*

*You could prepare a meal for someone who needs a break.
Or play a game of chess with your elderly neighbor.
Or maybe just linger for a while with your three-year-old,
playing his or her favorite game for the millionth time.*

*Don't despise the ordinary, the mundane, or the common.
More often than not, that's where God is hiding.*

• • •

Do not be anxious about anything,
but in every situation,
by prayer and petition,
with thanksgiving,
present your requests to God.

(Philippians 4:6)

• • •

DAY 17

HOW GOD SEES YOU

BEN WAS BLIND FROM THE DAY HE WAS BORN. Most people blamed his condition on Ben's parents. Some blamed him for his own blindness. For his entire life, Ben lived with the weight of physical darkness as well as the kind of darkness that comes with deep shame.

Ben never gazed up at the clouds trying to spot animal shapes. When others talked about the amazing colors of the rainbow, Ben had no way of even imagining what it was like. He had never seen the face of his mother, the smile of a child, or green grass in the springtime.

Ben knew the world only through sound and touch and taste. He had a sense of what things "looked like," but only in his mind's eye.

Because he had no way to work, Ben's life was relegated to begging just to stay alive. As he sat on the familiar street corner with his hand out, groups of children came by and tapped him from behind, laughing as they teased him.

When stories of a miracle worker began to spread, something deep inside Ben stirred. At first just a thought, quickly dismissed. Then nagging questions. What if the things people said about this Jesus were true? What if life could be different for Ben?

One day, there was a commotion in the streets. People gathered, murmuring and then shouting. He heard their pounding footfalls on the road.

"He's coming," someone cried out. "The miracle worker from Nazareth is on His way here!"

Ben couldn't see the group of people walking down the street, but he sensed that the crowd was moving toward him. He felt the press of legs and arms and bodies surrounding him.

He struggled to his feet, using his cane as a brace, and moved toward the edge of the road. As he stepped out of the shadows of the building behind him, he felt the warmth of the sun on his face. The aroma of fresh bread wafted through the air.

People were talking all around him. He picked out a few words from their conversations.

Messiah.

Carpenter.

Disciples.

Healer.

Miracles.

Suddenly, the people around him stopped moving. The air grew thicker as bodies pressed in around him, pushing as if they were trying to look at something. The sound of footsteps stopped. Voices hushed. The group on the road stopped right in front of Ben.

"So Jesus," a man said, "here's a question for You. This man was born blind. Was it his sin or the sins of his parents that caused it to happen?"

The familiar weight of shame came crashing down on Ben again. He wanted to run, but something deep inside of him wouldn't let him.

Everyone was quiet as they waited for an answer.

"Neither this man nor his parents sinned."

The words hung in the air. Ben felt the weight of shame lifting off of him as if it were being washed away.

Then Jesus said, "While I am in the world, I am the light of the world" (John 9:5).

For the first time ever, Ben felt as though he could see—not with his eyes but with his heart. The darkness was gone. He knew nothing would ever be the same.

He wanted to go home right away and tell his family. But as he started to move, he felt something unexpected. A man's fingers, touching his eyes. For a moment, he lost his breath. But the tender touch could only have been from Jesus.

The man wiped something on his eyelids. Ben heard someone nearby whisper, "Mud." A warm sensation filled his eyes. The feeling of love and hope that flooded his heart was almost more than he could bear.

Tears mixed with the mud in his eyes. For his entire life, Ben had felt alone in a world of darkness. Then Jesus touched him. The teacher everyone had been talking about took time for *him*.

"Go, wash in the Pool of Siloam," Jesus said.

Ben didn't question. He knew he needed to wash the mud out of his eyes. With a smile, he turned, and using his cane, he made his way to the bathing pool. He found the water's edge, knelt down, cupped his hands, and washed his face. He sensed others around him, leaning toward him.

At first, the water was almost painfully hot. He squeezed his eyes shut. Then, slowly, he opened them. He tried to stand, but his legs gave way. He lifted his head. And laughed out loud.

He could see blue sky and white clouds. He turned and saw green grass and rich, brown dirt. He watched iridescent colors dance in the waters of the pool.

"I ... I ... I can see!" He stammered out the words.

People gathered around him and asked him who did it and how it happened. They wanted answers. They wanted an explanation. But Ben didn't have one. He looked at them, seeing faces for the first time in his life, and said, "All I know is that I was blind, but now I can see!" (See John 9:1–12.)

That's what Jesus does for us. It doesn't take a mental ascent in order for the things of God to be revealed to us. It doesn't take a carefully crafted argument or a compelling sermon. Sometimes it just takes God meeting us where we are and opening our eyes.

For Ben, sight came first on the inside and then on the outside. Jesus wants to lift the shame and guilt of our lives. He wants us to be free from the pain and hurt that blinds us to God's love. Jesus wants us to trust Him. To let Him step in and do what only He can do.

*In what areas have people made assumptions
about you that you've begun to believe?
What if, today, you could believe what Jesus has to say
about you? He wants to set you free and open your eyes
so that you too can say, "I was blind, but now I see!"*

*Jesus wants to change the way you see others,
the way you see yourself, and the way you see Him.*

DAY 18

BETTER

LIFE OF THE WORLD

SO WE COME TO A POINT IN OUR LIVES where we surrender our hearts to Jesus and choose to follow Him. Now what? Is our salvation simply insurance so that we don't end up spending eternity in hell? Is there more to the Christian life than just going through the motions, attending church and maybe telling a few others about Him? What are we supposed to do with the generative, transformative Spirit of God that's offered to us as believers?

Part of our purpose is to make the world a better place. As stewards of creation, we have a mandate to care for the world around us. As God's light-bearers, we have the amazing opportunity to bring His nature into the world and see His resurrection power go to work to change not just us, but the world around us.

For most of my life, I was told that Christianity is all about finding salvation through Jesus for myself and then getting as many other people as possible to find Jesus too. So I ended up on sort of a salvation safari, constantly looking for someone else to pick off.

Without a doubt, telling others about the gospel is part of our calling as Christ followers, but that's not the only reason we're here. We need to tell others about God's transformative love. But we are also meant to shine the light of God into our culture. Our purpose is not just to be part of God's mission to redeem others but also to engage in God's mission to redeem His world.

God wants us to reflect His glory in every part of our world, including education, business, government, social issues, and the arts. We shouldn't be content to hide in our corner of Christianity and thumb our noses at the rest of the world. We need to lead the way and bring God's light into every area of life.

For generations, Christianity led the way in the expression of the arts. During the Renaissance, Christians were the pioneers in music, writing, architecture, and theater. The early liturgy used story to tell the narrative of the Bible to people who couldn't read it. Stained glass was the fourteenth-century version of moving lights. For a large swath of history that started with the early church, Christians were at the front of the line, cutting a path with a Christ-inspired blade. But since the industrial revolution, we've handed things off to the rest of the world and been content to be imitators rather than initiators.

But Jesus said, "Let your light shine before others, that they may see your good deeds and glorify your Father in heaven" (Matthew 5:16). How do we do that? We make great artwork. We develop the best new business ideas. We prepare amazing meals. We revolutionize industries. We create films that are as beautiful as they are redemptive.

In the Old Testament, when the Israelites were in captivity, King Nebuchadnezzar recruited the best and brightest of the young men of Israel to serve in the palace. As part of their training, these men were educated in language, literature, and culture. The king observed that in every way, the Israelite men were "ten times" better than the other guys around them (Daniel 1:20).

It's been a long time since that's been the case for Christianity. But I think that's what God wants from us. He's not looking for us to hide from the world and wait for His return. He doesn't want us to just imitate what those around us create. He wants us to lead the way. He wants us, the ones who reflect His glory, to shape and care for culture, not react to it.

Christ followers should be the ones who find solutions to the world's hunger problems. We should be the ones who create economic freedom for people trapped in poverty. We should be the ones who win Oscars and Grammys and Nobel Peace Prizes and Pulitzer awards. Not for our glory, but for His. Jesus died on the cross and rose from the dead not just to give us resurrection life, but for us to be His hands and feet to bring that resurrection life to even the most lifeless parts of our culture.

In what ways have you been inspired to impact culture around you? In what ways have you been afraid of culture? How can you use your unique talents and abilities to make a positive impact on culture?

• • •

You are the salt of the earth.
But if the salt loses its saltiness,
how can it be made salty again?
It is no longer good for anything,
except to be thrown out and trampled
underfoot. You are the light of the world. A
town built on a hill cannot
be hidden. Neither do people light a
lamp and put it under a bowl. Instead they
put it on its stand, and it gives light to
everyone in the house. In the same way,
let your light shine before others,
that they may see your good deeds
and glorify your Father in heaven.

(Matthew 5:13–16)

Be perfect, therefore, as your
heavenly Father is perfect.

(Matthew 5:48)

• • •

DAY 19

LENS

HOW DO YOU SEE JESUS?

WHEN I WAS TWELVE, I WAS A BIT OF A SCIENCE NERD. My favorite magazines were *Popular Science, National Geographic,* and *Starlog.* And at this age, the only thing I wanted for Christmas was a telescope. I thought about it. I dreamed about it. And I knew exactly which one I wanted: the Jason 313 with three interchangeable eyepieces.

I woke up early on Christmas and ran downstairs, finding the box that I just knew contained that telescope. I ripped open the wrapping and the box, then spent an hour putting it together. I could hardly wait twelve hours for the sky to get dark.

Finally, I aimed my new telescope up and into the night. The moon hung bright in the sky. I couldn't wait to discover a new planet.

But as it turned out, the moon looked only slightly bigger than it did without the telescope. What I saw was a small, distorted image of the real thing. The infamous Jason 313 wasn't exactly the Hubble.

I also discovered that telescopes reverse everything so they appear upside down.

The main thing I ended up useing the telescope for was to spy on the neighbors. As they seemed to walk on the ceiling. Talk about expectations versus reality.

What lens do you see Jesus through?

A lens of religion?

A lens of doubt?

A lens of tradition?

How we see Jesus is one of the most important questions we can ask ourselves. Do you visualize Him as a little baby lying in a manger? Do you think of Him as a smiling, long-haired white man sitting on a rock, holding a lamb?

As "The Thorn" has grown through the years, it's been part of our mission to keep it real and not become "your grandma's passion play." We don't have Peter singing from the garden, no halo-wearing angels, and we don't wrap a blue sash around a white-robed Jesus.

Jesus wasn't at all what artists have painted Him to be. First of all, He wasn't dashingly handsome. You know all those pictures of Jesus with the perfect hair and high cheekbones and rosy cheeks? Forget about it. The Bible tells us that Jesus "had no form or majesty that we should look at him, and no beauty that we should desire him" (Isaiah 53:2 ESV). He wasn't perfect looking, didn't wear a sash, and probably didn't even have long hair. (That was considered shameful in Jesus' day.)

As far as looks go, Jesus was an everyman. Matter of fact, He was a man's man. Carpenters in Jesus' day couldn't drive to the Home Depot and pick up a truckload of two-by-fours. They cut the lumber they needed from fresh timber. Then they had to strip off bark, split the wood, and cut and shape it to fit the project.

Carpenters also had to work with stone. Not bricks or slabs of granite, but boulders that had to be chiseled. No doubt Jesus was strong from working with His hands every day. Calloused fingers, barrel chest, a steel grip. Gives a whole new meaning to the word *meek*. Strength under control—that was Jesus.

Jesus was a nonconformist. He wasn't Mr. Nice Guy. If anything, Jesus had a reputation for being a rebel. He was constantly challenging the religious elite. He healed on the Sabbath (which was against religious law). He wasn't super popular. If He'd lived today, He wouldn't have millions of YouTube hits or thousands of likes on Facebook.

Jesus was unpredictable. He was always surprising those around Him. The one who turned the tables in the temple told us to turn the other cheek. The one who walked on water walked right into the hands of His betrayer. The one who worked with wooden beams allowed Himself to be crucified on a cross.

Jesus was tough. His ministry was physically exerting. He sometimes walked twenty miles a day, spoke for hours at a time, and stayed to pray with people until the last one had left. On top of that, Jesus endured beating, flogging, trials, and the most brutal torture ever invented. He was no pansy.

Jesus wasn't afraid of His emotions. He wept, He longed, He anguished. He also had a great sense of humor and loved catching people by surprise. Like when He appeared to His disciples with no warning. And did the same thing with strangers on the way to Damascus. He should capture us by surprise too.

Jesus had a vivid personality.
He was a:
Storm walker
Pharisee challenger
Demon chaser
Underdog champion

How do you see Jesus?

DAY 20

CARRY

JESUS WANTS TO CARRY YOU

RICK HOYT WAS BORN IN 1962. Because he didn't get enough oxygen to his brain at birth, he was diagnosed as a spastic quadriplegic with cerebral palsy. Rick's parents, Dick and Judy Hoyt, were told that their son would never lead a normal life and that the best thing they could do for him was to send him to an institution to live out his days.

Dick and Judy were determined to give Rick as normal a life as they could. After they realized that Rick couldn't walk or speak, they began looking for other ways for him to communicate. In 1972, they worked with a group of engineers to create a special interactive computer that allowed Rick to spell out words. His first sentence was "Go Bruins!" No doubt he was a typical boy on the inside, even though he had severe physical limitations on the outside.

In 1977, Rick told his father that he wanted to participate in a five-mile benefit run for a lacrosse player who'd been paralyzed in an accident. Dick agreed to push Rick in his wheelchair. The two of them managed to go all five miles, finishing in next-to-last place. That night, Rick told his father, "Dad, when I'm running, it feels like I'm not handicapped."[3]

This event began an epic story of love and freedom. Over the past few decades, Team Hoyt has completed more than one thousand races, including the Boston Marathon and six Ironman triathlons. For the Ironman, Dick rides a special bike with a seat for Rick in the front. When swimming, Dick pulls his son in a specially made raft. In 1992, Dick and Rick biked and ran across the entire United States.

Rick was once asked, if he could give his father one thing, what would it be? Rick responded, "The thing I'd most like is for my dad to sit in the chair and I would push him for once." Talk about friendship. Talk about loyalty. Talk about love.

The Bible tells of a time when a group of friends did the same kind of thing for a member of their "band of brothers." While Jesus was preaching, a few men, wanting to get their paraplegic friend to Him, went to the extreme of climbing on top of the building that Jesus was preaching in and making a huge hole in the roof so they could lower their friend down with ropes (Mark 2:1–12).

The Bible doesn't tell us why this man was paralyzed or who his friends were. The man could have been in the military, injured

---

3 "About Team Hoyt," www.teamhoyt.com/About-Team-Hoyt.html.

in the heat of battle. Or he might have fallen at a worksite, screaming in pain as his colleagues lifted a giant boulder off of his crushed back. Or perhaps he was attacked by a wild animal on a hunting trip.

We do know the crippled man had friends, unlike a lot of other blind, crippled, or lame people Jesus encountered. In his day, disabled people were marginalized and denied access to many things everyone else enjoyed. But like Dick Hoyt, this man's buddies were determined. They carried their friend's mat, found a way through the crowd, scaled a building, demolished a roof, and rappelled him down to Jesus. Talk about commitment.

I love the faith of the crippled man. When Jesus told him to "rise, pick up your bed, and go home," he didn't hesitate.[4] I imagine he twisted and moved, and as he did, the bones in his body popped and snapped and clicked back into place. Imagine watching a paralyzed man suddenly sit up, touch his toes, and bend his knees.

I can see this guy thanking Jesus and then looking up and fist-pumping toward his friends, who were looking down at the drama below them.

That man would never have been able to get close to Jesus if someone hadn't carried him. And Rick Hoyt would never have felt the rush of air on his face if his father hadn't pushed him.

Near the end of the final book in the Lord of the Rings trilogy is a scene where Frodo and Samwise are trying to reach the mouth of Mount Doom in order to throw the dreaded Ring of Power into its molten fires. Totally exhausted, Frodo turns to Samwise and offers the ring to him, telling him that he can't go any farther. Samwise looks at his friend and says, "I can't carry your burden. But I can carry you."

---

4   Mark 2:11 ESV

God didn't create us to live life alone. We are designed to live in community. That's when we can do what Dick Hoyt did for his son. That's when we can do what Samwise did for Frodo. In community we can do for one another what Jesus has done for us. He carries us when we can't go on, so we can carry each other when the going gets tough.

Carrying someone might take the form of a phone call, a text, or a simple prayer. Or it might be a cup of coffee with a long conversation, or an intervention with others who also love like you do.

Pray, "God, show me who I can carry today," and then follow the Holy Spirit's lead.

• • •

Never will I leave you;
never will I forsake you.

(Hebrews 13:5)

• • •

DAY 21

LITTLE

WITH GOD, LITTLE BECOMES MUCH

SIMON HAD ALWAYS BEEN SMALL. His parents had named him after the great king of Israel, but he hardly fit the bill. In fact, he often wondered if his father would have been happier with a girl. That's what the other kids called him sometimes, especially during races.

It's not that he didn't try. He was just smaller than the other boys. His mother said he'd been born early because God couldn't wait for everyone to meet him. That always made him smile. He glanced over at her now as she packed his meal for the day. Five small barley loaves and two fish.

"A meal fit for a king," she said, beaming at her son. "I put a bit more in there than you'll need, in case anyone else is hungry."

Simon nodded as his mother handed him the meal in a basket. "Thanks."

A commotion outside meant that others were gathering to make the trip to hear the famous teacher from Nazareth. Word had spread that Jesus was going to be near the lake that afternoon. Simon had only seen Him once, before He was famous, at his cousin's wedding. Since then the news about Jesus had spread like crazy.

Simon joined the group. When they arrived at the lake, he couldn't believe his eyes. Other than the feasts in Jerusalem, he had never seen so many people in the same place. There had to be five or six thousand men sitting on the hillside overlooking the lake, along with countless women and children.

Several hours passed as if time were standing still. Simon was mesmerized by Jesus. Every word seemed to be spoken just for him.

When someone nearby whispered something about food, Simon realized that it was past dinnertime. His stomach grumbled. He may have been smaller than the other kids, but he'd always had a big appetite.

As Jesus continued teaching, one of His friends leaned over and said something to Him. Simon jostled a bit to get closer. Jesus smiled and said, "You feed them." The disciples looked confused. But a few moments later, they started wandering through the crowds.

One of the disciples, a man named Andrew, came near Simon. "Does anyone have any food?"

Without thinking, Simon jumped up. "I do!" Standing on his tiptoes, he struggled to be seen.

Andrew walked over to him. He was taller than he looked standing next to Jesus down by the water's edge. He knelt down. "What do you have, son?"

Simon reached into his basket and drew out the cloth that held the food his mother had packed. A little embarrassed, he said, "Just these loaves and fish."

Andrew smiled. "Thank you, but—"

As he said it, Jesus smiled and nodded, motioning as if to say, *Bring it here.*

"If Jesus wants my lunch," Simon said excitedly, "He can have it."

As Andrew walked away with his basket, Simon couldn't have been happier. The teacher wanted his lunch for Himself. What an honor!

Jesus took the little loaf, broke it, lifted it into the air, and blessed it. When He lowered Simon's little lunch basket, it looked as though there was more bread in it than Simon's mother had packed.

He had to be seeing things.

Jesus dumped the bread in Simon's basket into a larger basket. And then another. And another. The bread kept coming, as if his little basket was somehow making bread!

Simon remembered the story his father often told him about God raining down bread from heaven as the Israelites were leaving Egypt. Jesus was doing the same thing now!

The people closest to Jesus shouted and pointed. As the disciples started passing around the baskets of fish and bread, everyone praised God. Some laughed and danced. It was the biggest, most exciting feast Simon had ever seen.

"Thank you," Andrew said as he handed the little basket back to Simon.

For the first time in his life, Simon didn't feel small and weak and insignificant. He mattered. Jesus used what little he had to offer and turned it into much. Deep in his heart, Simon knew his life could be much too. God didn't see the size of his body but the size of his heart.[5]

That's how God works with us. When we feel inadequate or small or helpless, He steps in and reminds us that He is enough.

Jesus could have worked it out so that everyone was unexpectedly full or that the biggest caterer in Galilee just happened to show up at that very moment. But He didn't. God used this moment to remind us that in our weakness, He is strong. He is made bigger in our smallness.

That's the way God works. He loves to use the small or weak or seemingly insignificant things in our lives to surprise us and those around us.

A shepherd boy slays a giant.

A convict leads God's people from Egypt.

A tiny woman from Macedonia becomes Mother Teresa.

A few lyrics penned by a barroom singer become "How Great Thou Art."

God can use small beginnings, little talent, weak people. And with them, He will confound the wise and build His kingdom.

"Do you not know? Have you not heard? The Lord is the everlasting God, the Creator of the ends of the earth. He will not grow tired or weary, and his understanding no one can fathom. He gives strength to the weary and increases the power of the weak" (Isaiah 40:28–29).

---

5   Paraphrased from Mark 6:30–44.

In what areas of your life do you feel weak or insignificant? Today let your prayer be "Lord, in my weakness You are strong."

DAY 22

STORM

JESUS IS THERE IN THE MIDST OF THE STORM

THERE ARE TIMES IN LIFE WHEN WE CAN SEE JESUS CLEARLY. Days when it seems like He's right there with us. Moments when it feels like, if we wanted to, we could reach out and touch Him, as if He's sitting across the table.

But there are other days when He feels far away or when we lose sight of Him altogether. What was once a clear view of Jesus turns into a blurry outline and then, sometimes, into nothing at all. And we're left asking questions. Where is Jesus when ...

my marriage is falling apart?

my business is facing disaster?

my daughter doesn't come home?

my friend is diagnosed with cancer?

I think that's how the disciples felt when they learned that Herod had beheaded John the Baptist.[6]

Jesus loved John. When the whiplash of grief struck Him that day, He looked for a place to get away. But He couldn't find one. As many as twenty-five thousand people had followed Jesus and knew where He was. So He put His own emotions on hold as He preached and healed and loved them. And the disciples managed the crowd.

When the service would normally have been over so everyone could get dinner, the disciples encouraged Jesus to send the crowds away. I imagine the Twelve were tired and ready to move on. But not Jesus. In spite of what must have been swirling emotions, He found a way to feed them instead of ending the meeting. He turned a few loaves of bread and fish into enough food to feed a stadium of people.

As the meeting lingered on into the evening, I imagine one of the disciples leaning toward Jesus and saying, "Master, we have an appointment on the other side of the sea tomorrow morning. We need to leave soon if we want make it in time." Jesus basically told the disciples to go on ahead and He'd find a way to meet them there. (And did He ever!)

The disciples rigged up the boat, shoved off the shore, and headed to the opposite side of the Sea of Galilee. I wonder if any of them looked at Jesus, still taking time with the lingerers on the seashore, and said, "You know, we probably should have just waited for Him." But these guys were tired from a long day of ministry. They weren't thinking about keeping Jesus near. They were probably looking forward to being away from people and to getting a little shut-eye on the cruise.

---

6   Mark 6:26–29.

If they got any sleep at all, it didn't last long. During the night, the sea erupted and the clouds burst into a fury. For hours, the disciples worked the rigging and the sails and the oars, straining to keep the boat upright. Perhaps also straining to see where Jesus was. After all, He'd promised to meet them. He had to be on the way. But where was He? The coast had disappeared and, with it, any sign of the one they'd left everything to follow.

They were alone and afraid.[7]

Have you ever felt that way? Like one moment you are safe in the presence of God and the next you're out in the middle of a storm, all on your own? I've felt that way.

In 2011, Sarah and I decided to launch "The Thorn" as a national tour. We made all the preparations, booked the venues, recruited the team, and jumped on the bus. The tour was amazing! Like the multiplication of the bread and fish, crowds packed in to see "The Thorn." It was an overwhelming success. Until the tour was over.

Once the dust settled and the last truck was unpacked, and Sarah and I were left alone in a cramped warehouse, we realized that the inaugural Thorn tour had been a spiritual mountaintop but a financial disaster. For the next three years, we found ourselves in the middle of a storm unlike anything we'd experienced before.

A loss of more than $500,000 left us with mounting bills, threats of foreclosure, and lots of embarrassing conversations. For the first time in our lives, we were dependent on friends for groceries and gas money. I could really relate to the disciples who were in the boat that night. The joy and amazement of feeding the thousands was being overshadowed by the gripping fear of the storm. The sounds of cheering crowds had been drowned out by the crashing waves and booming thunder.

---

7   Mark 6:45–52.

I really wanted to quit. Where was Jesus? Had He forgotten me? Had He abandoned me?

As the disciples struggled in the boat that night, Jesus was praying on the other side of the lake. He understood what they were going through. His watchful eyes had never left them. He realized the value of keeping the faith and pressing through the storm. He knew these were the men who would birth the early church. And they would face storms much fiercer and more poorly timed than this one. They needed to learn to trust Him. Paul, who would join their ranks later, would learn that same lesson in his own storm at sea.

That's what Jesus taught me too. In those years following the national tour of "The Thorn," Sarah and I learned to press into Jesus. We kept moving forward. We trusted Him to bail us out when everything around was threatening to drown us. And you know what? He did. Not overnight and not like a lottery. It took a long time, but eventually the storm subsided.

When I looked up and searched the horizon, I saw something. As I looked more closely, I saw someone walking toward me. A man. No, more than a man. And He was coming for me. I collapsed and fell into His arms. And those arms, with one motion, caused the waves to stop and the rain to subside.

Have there been times in your life when you wanted to give up on God? He's never given up on you. Today, whatever your circumstances, look to God for strength and courage.

• • •

Be strong and do not give up,
for your work will be rewarded.

(2 Chronicles 15:7)

• • •

99

DAY 23

TAXED

GOD OFFERS YOU A FRESH START

NO ONE IS BORN WITH A BAD
REPUTATION.

Some of us might be born with a bad
name—imagine being a relative of Hitler or the
grandson of Mussolini or one of Idi Amin's daughters.
But it takes time to build a reputation.

As hours turn into days and days weave together into years,
people make judgments about you. Then one day, you realize that
others are making decisions based on your reputation.

"Don't do business with him. He's a financial wreck."

"Don't trust her. She'll stab you in the back."

"Don't date him. He'll love you and leave you."

"Don't let your kids hang out at their house."

"Don't tell her something unless you want the world to know about it."

I wonder what people would have said about Matthew. After all, he was a tax collector. As bad a rap as the IRS gets today, it's nothing compared to the way tax men were seen in Jesus' time.

Tax collectors were basically the biblical equivalent of the mob, known for gouging people as they collected taxes for their Roman bosses. To say that they were hated by the religious elite would be an understatement.

I imagine that if the pre-Jesus Matthew were alive today, he'd be the sort of guy who would come over to my house, shred my 1099 and my schedule C, and ask for more money than I really owed. He'd probably walk out of my house with my prized espresso machine, and if I complained, he'd send the local Roman head-cracker after me.

The Bible doesn't tell us how Matthew ended up sitting behind a tax collector's table. Maybe he'd started running with the wrong friends as a teenager and Dad kicked him out of the house. Perhaps he owed a gambling debt and had no choice but to work it off for "the man."

Whatever the circumstances, something kept him from following the normal path of school and apprenticeship. Something that he'd done, or that was done to him, had derailed him from what was considered a respectable career.

Over the years, Matthew had learned to endure the scowls and sideways glances and whispered gossip. He was used to it. He'd learned to accept who he was.

A thief.

A crook.

DAY 23

A mobster.

A reject.

Then one day, the noise of the square suddenly died down. Matthew looked up and saw a group of men walking toward him. Someone whispered the name Jesus. He'd never heard of Him. Behind Jesus was a handful of religious leaders, walking with arms folded and eyes pinched, waiting like hyenas.

Matthew knew what they were thinking. He'd heard it a thousand times. Here was a rich, happy, powerful tax collector. They were all watching, sneering, waiting for this rabbi to put Matthew in his place.

Let the circus begin.

It wouldn't be the first time he'd been verbally accosted by the religious leaders and probably not the last. To be honest, he deserved it in a way. After all, he wasn't exactly a Boy Scout. Like the other tax collectors, he took a little off the top.

As Jesus drew closer to Matthew, the rabbi's eyes caught him by surprise. He felt as if those eyes could see right through him, into his very soul.

When Jesus stopped in front of Matthew's table, he almost burst into tears. But instead of picking up the broken pieces of Matthew's life and showing them to everyone, Jesus was some-how *mending* them.

In that moment, it was as if the weight of thirty-six years was lifted from him. Like a wave of forgiveness was washing over his heart, all the bitterness and hurt was being pushed down-stream. The chains he'd grown used to were broken. The pain he'd learned to live with was gone.

What was this? *Who* was this?

"Follow Me," Jesus said.

Everyone gasped as if the air had been sucked out of the square. No one spoke. Then whispers began. Religious leaders leaned in toward one another, with gaping eyes and pointing fingers. It was one thing for Jesus to touch the unclean or to preach about giving to the poor. But it was another thing entirely for Him to ask someone who was clearly a sinner to follow Him.

In that moment, Matthew realized that Jesus was willing to risk His reputation on a bottom-of-the-barrel guy like him and actually lift him up. With those two words, Jesus was saying that He accepted Matthew and that He was willing to offer him all the benefits of being associated with a rabbi. For Matthew, it was the ultimate do-over.

A clean slate.

A fresh start.

That's what Jesus offers to you and me too. No matter what we've done or where we've been, He gives us a chance for a brand-new beginning. A chance to reboot our lives. And He doesn't just say our past is forgiven. He lends us His reputation. He clothes us in His righteousness. And there's nothing we can do to earn it. We don't have to be perfect. All we have to do is follow.

A reputation takes years to create, but Jesus can change our lives in a moment.

Is your reputation holding you back from moving into God's design for your life? Today, put away your old self and take on His righteousness.

DAY 24

FORGIVEN

YOU ARE FORGIVEN AND LOVED

DO YOU KNOW WHAT IT FEELS LIKE TO GET CAUGHT? I've been caught speeding, sneaking food during a diet, and cheating on a spelling test when I was a kid. (Turns out the ink wouldn't just wipe off my arm like my friend Jeff said it would.) For you, maybe it was a lie you couldn't back out of or a text message you wish you'd deleted. There's nothing like the heart-sinking feeling of staring at someone you care about and fumbling for words as your heart tumbles inside you.

The woman in John 8:1–11 felt like that.

She was probably already feeling bad about herself, a shadow of the promising young girl she'd been in her childhood. As she closed the door and prepared for yet another encounter with a man who wasn't her husband, the door to her heart closed with it.

As her next meal ticket starts having his way with her, a loud bang sounds from outside the room. Shouts. Accusations. Angry words. The man she's with flushes with fear, yanks open a back door, and dashes safely into the shadows. Her reaction is slower, like moving through sand. But she manages to slip out the back door as the front door crashes open, splinters flying.

Half naked, she runs as far and as fast as she can and then realizes she went the wrong way. She spins around—too quickly. White-hot pain pulses through her as she crashes to the dirt. Dust flies into her mouth, her eyes. She covers her face and tucks her knees to her chest.

She swallows hard and prays under her breath, like she did when she was a child, even though she knows God doesn't hear her.

Men's voices surround her, shouting.

A rock slams into her back. She cries out in pain. She is being stoned.

This is how her life will end. Lying on a dusty street, angry men all around her. With eyes shut tight, she whispers another prayer.

Silence falls. The rock pelting stops. She looks up. All eyes are focused behind her. Another accuser, no doubt.

She drops her face to the ground, waiting for the next stone. Instead, someone gently drapes a garment over her bare skin, hiding her shame. Slowly peering up, she sees the back of a man, kneeling down, writing in the dust. A murmur reverberates around her as the rabble stirs. She strains to read the writing, but it's obscured by the heat of the sun and the silhouette of this man who has waded into her moment of shame.

He rises, and without looking at her, calls out, "The one of you who is without sin, throw the first stone."

She tenses. But nothing happens.

The man's dusty feet under a weathered robe stand directly in her path. Who is He? She suddenly has an overwhelming need to see His face. But she doesn't dare meet His gaze.

Seconds pass and everyone remains still. Then a stone drops out of someone's hand. Pools of dust spring up from the ground as one by one the accusers release their rocks back to the earth.

Within minutes the square is vacant. Clutching the tunic around her, she gazes up at Jesus. He looks at her with love and compassion so direct and exacting that it seems to invade every part of her.

"Who is condemning you?" He asks.

She looks around but already knows that no one is there. She meets His gaze again, not wanting to experience another moment without this compassion. "No one is here to condemn me."

Jesus smiles. "Then I don't condemn you either."

He takes her hand and lifts her to her feet. His touch is firm yet gentle and fatherly.

"Now, go and live your life," He says. "But do not sin again."

That encounter with Jesus changed this woman. One moment, she was as good as dead. The next, she was free and filled with the hope that life could be different.

Have you ever felt like the adulteress woman, caught and cornered? Maybe your mistakes and flaws aren't public and on display for everyone around you. Or maybe they are. But if you're like me, there are days when you feel as if the Enemy is walking in circles around you, reminding you of all the mistakes you've made and the person you used to be, lying to you about who you are, threatening to destroy you, hoping you'll just give up.

The accuser reminds you that you slipped up again. Even after vowing that you won't do it anymore, he tells you it'll happen again tomorrow. He whispers that you'll never be a good friend or that you'll always be an addict or that you haven't really changed. This faith thing isn't worth it. It's not for you. You're not good enough. And you never will be.

But Jesus doesn't condemn you. He doesn't see you for who you are on your worst days. He loves you deeply and forgives completely. He never looks backward. Instead, He kneels in front of you, in the heat of your worst decisions and failures and flaws, and He offers His hand, full of forgiveness and hope and newness.

Will you accept His free gift of forgiveness?

Now that you have been set free from sin and have become slaves of God, the benefit you reap leads to holiness, and the result is eternal life.

• • •

For the wages of sin is death,
but the gift of God is eternal life
in Christ Jesus our Lord.

(Romans 6:22–23)

• • •

DAY 25

AGAIN

FOR GOD SO LOVED YOU

IT WAS NOT AN EASY DECISION. I imagine Nicodemus went back and forth in his head, trying to decide whether or not he should meet with Jesus. After all, Nicodemus was a member of the most rigid group of religious leaders, the Sanhedrin. The same guys who had plotted the beheading of John the Baptist and were working hard to find a way to trap Jesus so they could arrest Him.

But no matter how much he wanted to, he couldn't deny the reports he'd heard and what he'd seen for himself. The blind saw. The lame walked. Regular water turned into the finest wine. One fish turned into sushi for thousands. There was no way Jesus could do what He did unless God was with Him.

He knew that much. And He had to know more.

So he arranged a meeting with Jesus on the outskirts of town, under the cover of trees and shadows. But this was more than just a meeting between two men. It was a clash of ideas. Nicodemus believed that what people did drew them close to God. Jesus believed that only He could draw a person to God.

All his life, Nicodemus had been about works. Jesus was all about unearned forgiveness. On one side was legalism, where it was up to human beings to be good enough to please God. On the other side was grace, where salvation had nothing to do with us—that was God's job. He offered it, according to Jesus, not to the select few who belonged to the right group and did the right things, but to everyone.

One question kept nagging Nicodemus. Why would God offer such an important gift to just anyone? Why would He offer a clean slate and new life to the sick, the sinner, the Samaritan?

That night, Nicodemus found out that the answer was simple.

Love.

The words Jesus spoke to Nicodemus have been etched from the heart of God into the hearts of billions. If you grew up in church, you know the verse. It was the first Bible verse I memorized. If you've watched an NFL game, you've seen the reference written on signs and drawn on player's cheeks.

They are the most important words ever written.

The ultimate declaration of independence.

The greatest pardon offered in all of history.

The words have been printed on more pages and preached in more sermons than any other in all of Christendom. If you were to interview people on the street and ask them, this would be the most quoted verse in all the Bible.

"For God *so loved* the world that he gave his one and only Son, that whoever believes in him shall not perish but have eternal life" (John 3:16, emphasis added).

Like a governor calling in a pardon at 11:59 p.m., these words offer hope when there is none to be found. They are like a lighthouse on a stormy sea, beckoning all who see it to come near and avoid the peril that lies around them.

Nicodemus must have been surprised by this response. It was the opposite of what he'd been taught his entire life. There was no code to follow. No secret handshake that showed you were part of the club. There were no rules that had to be followed in order to measure up. And it wasn't just for a select few. Salvation was for everyone.

Under the Old Testament law, the only way to have hope for the forgiveness of sins was to offer a sacrifice. The bigger the sin, the bigger the sacrifice. In order to stay in favor with God, you had to follow the law and then hope that you were good enough.

But none of us can do that. How good is good enough? No one knows. The only sacrifice that was big enough to cover our sin, make us clean, and give us new life is the sacrifice of Jesus.

For God so loved.

I wonder what was going through Nicodemus's head when Jesus told him this. Here was a guy who had tried to do everything right. As a religious leader, he knew the Scriptures. He taught them. He knew exactly which things to do and which things not to do. He had learned to measure himself and others against the impossibly high standards of the law. His entire life, he'd had to bear the weight of being judge and jury. But God never designed any of us to do that.

What Jesus offered Nicodemus that day was something no one had ever offered him before. Freedom.

For the first time in his life, Nicodemus felt the shackles of judgment fall from his heart. The vice grip of legalism was loosened and his soul could breathe freely. It felt like coming up for air after struggling underwater for a long time. His new heart was so full of God's love and grace that nothing else mattered.[8]

We know that this encounter with Jesus changed Nicodemus because the Bible tells us that after Jesus died, he boldly asked for the body so that he could anoint it and bury it. He didn't care what anyone else thought anymore. He was free, once and for all. He was loved. And no matter what he did or didn't do, nothing could change that.

Does God love you? Yes! How much does He love you? Enough to send His one and only Son to take your place.

Never forget that.

Would you pray with me?

Dear God, thank You for loving me so much
that You sent Jesus to take my place.
Today, I again surrender my will to Yours
and I accept Your love for me.
Forgive me for trying to take my life into my own hands.
I realize that I can never earn Your love
but that You have freely given it to me.

---

8   John 3:1–15.

DAY 25

DAY 26

PRAY

JESUS MODELED PRAYER FOR YOU

AS A YOUTH PASTOR, I USED TO TEACH TEENS something I called the three-legged stool. The idea was that it took all three legs of the stool to avoid the penalty of gravity. If any of the legs were pulled out, you'd fall. The same is true about our Christian life.

One of the legs on the stool is time in the Word of God. King David said, "Your word is a lamp for my feet, a light on my path" (Psalm 119:105). I've navigated enough nighttime mountain trails and dark, LEGO-scattered hallways to know the importance of light.

The second leg on the stool is time with other believers. Paul wrote to the church, "Encourage one another and build each other up, just as in fact you are doing" (1 Thessalonians 5:11). None of us is meant to live life as an island; rather, we should act like mountain climbers, with at least one person above us, pulling us up, and another person below us whom we're pulling up.

Time with God is the final leg on the stool. Prayer may be one of the most misunderstood aspects of the Christian walk. Over the years, we've overhyped it, undersold it, mystified it, and ignored it. At its simplest, prayer is communication with God, and it usually comes in the form of "help," "thanks," and awe.

Perhaps the most sincere prayer we can pray is "God, help me."

Help me get out of this mess.

Help me make the right decisions.

Help me endure the next chemo treatment.

Help me love my wife.

Help me get back on track.

I think sometimes we feel like "help me" prayers are selfish and that God frowns at the disproportionate amount of them we shoot up to Him. Truth is, God wants genuine prayers more than anything, and when we're praying "help me" prayers, they're usually from our deepest self.

And we're not alone in this.

Jonah prayed from the belly of the whale (Jonah 2:1).

The Hebrew boys prayed from the fiery furnace (Daniel 3:17–28).

Solomon prayed for wisdom (2 Chronicles 1:10–12).

Hannah prayed for a child (1 Samuel 1:10–11).

When God answers a "help me" prayer, the next thing we do is offer a "thank you" prayer.

If you're a parent, one of the main things you want from your kids is gratitude. Now that I have kids, I know why my parents were constantly saying, "All we want are grateful children."

God wants the same thing from us. Has God blessed you? Do you have a good marriage, happy children, decent health, a roof over your head, arms and legs that work like they were designed to? Do you have enough to eat and a job that pays most of the bills? Do you have the freedom to worship God and own a Bible? If you can say yes to even one of these things, you've got something to be thankful for.

The Psalms are full of David's thankfulness to a God who redeems the past and paves a new future. Thankfulness to a God who forgives and forgets and forges a new life for us in Him. Now, that's something to be thankful for.

Please.

Thank you.

What else can we say?

As a kid, my dad always corrected me when I used the word *awesome* as a colloquialism. You know, like, "Dude, that's awesome!" He'd always ask me, "Is that really awesome? Does it inspire awe? Does it make you speechless in rapt attention?" Uh ... no. But I'll tell you what does.

The way a baby forms in a mother's womb.

The vast distance between galaxies.

The towering height of a Colorado fourteener.

The brilliant colors of the Great Barrier Reef.

Quantum physics, string theory, photosynthesis, the cardio-vascular system, aerodynamics ... the list is endless.

Help. Thanks. Awe.

Jesus modeled the importance of prayer. When He wasn't answering the petitions of those around Him or teaching His disciples how to pray, He was stealing away to pray Himself. Jesus prayed in the wilderness, in the garden of Gethsemane, at the Last Supper, and on the cross of Calvary. Jesus was in constant communication with His Father. He talked with Him when He was hungry, tired, lonely, and struck with grief.

If it's good enough for Jesus,
it's definitely good enough for me.
Is it good enough for you?

DAY 27

FIERCE

JESUS WILL DEFEND YOU

GOD WANTS ALL HUMAN BEINGS TO FIND A WAY TO HIM. He doesn't want anything to get in the way of people discovering the grace and hope and life that's found in His Son, Jesus.

I think this is why, in the middle of what had been a pretty exciting and inspirational day, Jesus' emotions suddenly turned.

For the previous few hours, Jesus and the Twelve had been making their way through the streets of Jerusalem. People were packed everywhere—on the sides of the road, in trees, in windows. They were shouting, "Hosanna," waving palm branches, and laying down their coats so that the hooves of the colt Jesus was riding didn't touch the dirt. Talk about a celebrity entrance.

Jesus and His men wove their way through the city, heading to the spiritual center of Jerusalem, the temple. They walked through the great entry and into the temple courtyard, where people offered sacrifices in order to go farther into the temple and, presumably, get closer to God. Non-Jews weren't allowed to go farther because of the graven images on most currency.

In the outer courtyard, money changers sold animals to the people, some of whom were very poor. It must have been a pitiful sight as hundreds of people arrived at the temple, some after traveling many miles and days, only to realize that they couldn't afford to go into the temple.

Since this courtyard was the only place of worship accessible to the non-Jews, their entire community was forced to worship the Lord in the chaos of a makeshift market. Imagine if the church next door to yours set up a café in the middle of your worship service. People would be constantly jostling past you to order lattes and bacon-wrapped breakfast sandwiches while you're trying to pray and worship. Now multiply that by the sound and smell of goats!

The scene broke Jesus' heart. It also infuriated Him. It was bad enough that humanity had suffered throughout history since the garden of Eden. It was bad enough that people had been plagued with death and starvation and disease. But now, the ones who were *so loved* by God were being denied the most important liberty of all: access to His presence!

The Bright and Morning Star would have nothing of the darkness that is religious piety and spiritual abuse.

The carpenter-King burst into action, splintering tables that

He might have built Himself.[9] I wish I could have been there, as a wide-eyed spectator, watching the whirlwind of robe and hair and hands.

Jesus' message that day? Don't mess with My children. Don't you dare keep the ones who need to reach Me from getting there. The scene was heaven's version of the older brother stepping onto the playground, marching over to the bully, and socking him in the eye.

The Gospels tell of a handful of moments when Jesus got upset, and nearly every time His anger was directed at the religious leaders. Contrary to what some modern culture shapers would say, it wasn't because Jesus was against the idea of religion. Far from it. He loves the church. No, His wrath arose against these men for creating unneeded barriers that made it harder for His children to come near to God.

Imagine you have a child who wants to come into the house and be with you. Maybe she wants to apologize for something. Or she's hurt and needs your help. Perhaps she just wants your company. But someone is standing outside telling her that she hasn't met some arbitrary requirements, so she cannot see you. How would you respond?

In that moment in the temple, the Lord in human form responded like a loving father. He took a stand as the protector of the lowly and marginalized. And with the fierceness of a shot-gun-cleaning Texas father on prom night, He put the "fear of God" into these abusers.

The Son of God removed the barriers for His children and drove the oppressors away. The poor and the foreigner alike could now run to God in peace. No more men standing in their way or holding religious elitism over them.

---

9   Luke 19:28–48.

One week later Jesus went all the way and obliterated every barrier between mankind and the Father. He became the final sacrifice and threw open the door for us to come directly into His presence.

That is the kind of God we serve. One who not only looks out for His children but defends them like a lion protects its cubs.

Since Jesus has crushed the barriers, is there anything stopping you from running to the Father? Are you putting up barriers for yourself, or worse, for others? When Jesus toppled the temple tables two thousand years ago and set the doves and goats fleeing out of the temple like a scene from *Jumanji*, He made it pretty clear how He felt about spiritual blockades. So stop making your own. The Father's arms are open.

It's time to start running.

* * *

He himself is our peace,
who has made the two groups
one and has destroyed the barrier,
the dividing wall of hostility.

(Ephesians 2:14)

* * *

DAY 28

SMALL

COME TO JESUS LIKE A CHILD

HAVE YOU EVER NOTICED HOW AN-NOYING other people's children can be? When our own kids make noise or run around the store or throw food in public, we have this sort of mutant superpower that enables us to deal with it. But when other people's children misbehave in public, that's another story.

A while back, I invited a friend out to lunch to have a serious conversation. We sat in the booth, talking in low tones because we each wanted to convey to the other how important this conversation was. Suddenly, a sound like a combination between a screaming banshee and a dying coyote erupted from a booth near ours.

Lo and behold, two moms on a lunch date had come into the restaurant with two little kids in tow. Now, I'm not saying these kids were left totally to their own devices while the moms talked, seemingly oblivious to Hurricane Toddler that had just made landfall. But I'm not saying they weren't.

My friend and I scowled and cleared our throats and murmured until finally one of the moms noticed us. Embarrassed, she worked for the rest of the meal to manage those kids.

I was grateful that the rest of our lunch was much more peaceful. But I also realized how unlike Jesus I had become in that moment.

One day, when Jesus was in the middle of teaching, something made a ruckus in the crowd. People started to shift and whisper and shush. Then people started shushing the people who were shushing. Some folks pointed to the commotion. Suddenly, a clump of little children came bursting out of the standing throng and into the open area where Jesus stood.

One of the little boys ran up to Jesus and tried to swing from His arm. A little girl tugged on His robe and another pulled His shawl out from around His neck. The rest of the kids giggled and laughed and danced in excitement.

The adults instantly became uncomfortable. *Where are these kids' parents? Someone needs to teach them some manners. Seriously, this is a rabbi. Who's in charge of these unruly monsters?*

An old woman accompanied the kids—their babysitter or teacher. She meekly looked at Jesus and mumbled something about Him blessing the children. Finally, one of the disciples walked up and shooed them off, telling them not to bother the Master. The crowd gave a sigh of relief. A few raised a quiet cheer.

Then Jesus did what no one expected. He stopped His

disciples from shooing away the kids. He gave them a big smile—the kind with the warmth of a thousand suns.

"Let the children come to me," He said, "and do not hinder them, for the kingdom of God belongs to such as these" (Mark 10:14).

He prayed for them and blessed them.

At that point, I imagine that Jesus took a moment to play with the kids. The Bible doesn't say that, but it's so like His character. I can just see the little boy riding on His back and the little girl being swung in a circle, laughing like she was the only kid in the world. And when it was all over, I can hear all the kids saying, "Do it again! Again! Again!"

And I think He did it again.

That's the way Jesus is. Throughout the Bible, there are stories that show how much Jesus loves children. And when we love kids the way He did, when we care for them the way He did, that penetrates God's heart like nothing else.

When they were little, my five kids all loved being carried and held. It made them feel safe and loved. Sometimes I'd ask them what kind of "airplane ride" they wanted. A jet board? A helicopter? An upside down, inside out? Or maybe they wanted the granddaddy of all rides, the ultimate combo of all the different types of airplane rides I could think of. The one where I held them and spun them, turned them upside down and swung them around, all while running through the house. You know, safe dad stuff.

When it was over, my youngest daughter, Alison, would inevitably say, "Again, again, again."

That's how God sees us, His children. He loves it when we take care of little ones, but He also loves it when we come to Him like kids. After all, the kingdom of heaven is made of people "such as these."

Such as what? Quick to forgive. Easy to laugh. Unashamed to dance. Happy to see the Father's face. God wants us to leap into His arms, knowing that He loves being with us.

In what ways can you love children like Jesus did?
How can you come to God like a child today?
Maybe you need to remember how to laugh, how to smile,
how to tug on His sleeve and just ask Him to hold you.

He's always happy to.

DAY 29

SLEEP

JESUS WAITS FOR YOU

SOMETHING WAS DIFFERENT ABOUT THIS NIGHT.

The air was crisp, the moon was bright, and Peter was trying desperately to understand what was happening. He lingered close to Jesus as the disciples moved through the darkened streets, leaving the City of David and climbing to the top of the nearby hillside. As they walked, they offered up a hymn, a song of aching beauty that echoed all around them.

The Mount of Olives stood as a sentinel, towering over the Kidron Valley and overlooking the holy city of Jerusalem as it had for centuries. Thousand-year-old olive trees twisted their way up from the ground, as if determined to find sunlight and to remind everyone who saw them that they had endured even the hardest things in order to bear fruit and do what they were created to do.

The punishing desert sun had long since disappeared and had been replaced by the moon, which now lit up the garden in silver shards that cut between the branches of the ancient trees. The temperature had dropped and a mist now hovered above the ground, lending an eerie quality to this place that had been used as a graveyard for generations of people eagerly awaiting the return of the King.

Deep in the shadows between the trees, the disciples followed Jesus until they came to what had become a familiar place for them. A garden where the Master often went to pray. Three years ago, they had left their nets, closed their stores, and abandoned their tax collection booths in order to walk in the steps of their Rabbi. But tonight Peter sensed that this coming week would be some kind of culmination of what they had all been living for.

Hints of what was to come had been given—during the Master's talks, in conversations as they walked, even during the meal they had shared earlier that night.

Jesus turned to Peter, James, and John and asked them to walk with Him a little farther. While the others huddled together, quietly talking and singing songs, the chosen three followed Jesus to a garden. After asking them to wait there and pray for Him, Jesus went off a short distance to speak with His heavenly Father.

As the moon rose higher in the night sky, the singing was replaced with silence. The disciples fell asleep. Peter tried to stay awake, but his eyes grew heavy. He lay his head against a rock to rest.

A sound echoed in the olive grove.

Peter's eyes fluttered open. He sat up. Peering through the haze, he counted the sleeping disciples. Only eleven, including himself. Who was missing? As his memory returned from the fog of sleep, he remembered. Judas had left during the meal earlier, after an odd exchange with Jesus.

And where was Jesus? Peter shook his head. Only moments before—or was it hours?—Jesus had asked them to wait and pray for Him. As Peter whispered a prayer, his head wobbled and eventually found its way back to the rock.

"Peter, James, John!" a voice cried out of the darkness.

Peter jolted awake. James and John were already sitting up. Jesus stood in front of them. "Could you not keep watch with Me for one hour?"

Peter and John looked at each other, embarrassed.

"Watch and pray that you may not enter into temptation," Jesus continued, His voice filled with compassion. "The spirit indeed is willing, but the flesh is weak."

Peter, James, and John all asked for forgiveness. Then Jesus walked back to His place of prayer.

Why is He so intense tonight? Peter wondered as he settled back against the rock.

The other two lay their heads down, whispering prayers until they became mumbles and then nothing at all.

Peter stared at the night sky, looking through the branches and into the light of the moon. Earlier that night Jesus had predicted that Peter would deny Him.

"It'll never happen," he'd vowed.

Peter drifted off to sleep again. Jesus came back to check on His disciples three times, and each time He found them sleeping.[10]

When I think of Peter, James, and John trying desperately to

10   See Mark 14:32–42.

stay awake but giving in to sleep, I can't help but think of myself. How many times has Jesus asked even the simplest thing of me, and I responded with an exuberant "Yes!" but then failed to follow through? A willing spirit but a weak flesh. It has happened to me more times than I can count.

I don't think Jesus was asking His friends to pray in order to bolster His own prayers. Jesus didn't need that. I don't think Jesus asked them to pray with Him so that they would know how important prayer was. They already knew. I think Jesus asked them to pray with Him because He wanted them to be *with Him.*

The other day, I asked one of my daughters, Katherine, to come along with me on a few errands. We jumped into my truck, and for a few minutes we chatted about this and that. Then it got quiet. At first I thought I should fill the dead space and ask her about her day, her pets, or her thoughts. But then I figured I'd just let us be together, without having to say anything. To just be present.

After a few minutes, Katherine looked at me and said, "Dad, do you know what I like about hanging out with you?"

"What?"

"We don't always have to talk. But I know you love me, and I love you too." She scooted closer to me and wrapped her arm around mine. We sat that way, in silence, until we got to the pet store. And on the way home she talked and talked and talked.

Isn't that what Jesus really wants of us? He isn't looking for perfection or performance. He doesn't want perfect prayers or a certain number of minutes of dedicated, outlined time. He simply wants us to want to be with Him. God created you and me to be in relationship with Him. Prayer, in its simplest form, is us saying to God, *I want to be with You.*

DAY 29

Today, Jesus is saying,
"Will you spend some time with Me?"

Even though, like Peter, we fail more times than we
succeed, Jesus loves us and believes in us. He is waiting
for us to get up from where we are, move to where He is,
and then just sit by Him. We don't necessarily have to say
anything. We can just be with Him.

And that's enough.

DAY 30

FINISHED

SUBMIT YOUR WILL TO GOD'S WILL

AS THE DISCIPLES LAY ASLEEP NEAR-BY, JESUS PRAYED. Blood-filled tears rolled down His face as the Lion of Judah strained between heaven and earth. His words that night were sincere, spoken from the one who was as much man as He was God.

"My Father," He cried out, "if it is possible, may this cup be taken from me" (Matthew 26:39).

In His divinity, Jesus knew that His life would be offered up as a sacrifice for all of humanity. As a man, He wanted a way out. As God, He was willing to endure what lay ahead. As a man,

He hoped for another way, a last-minute pardon. A ram in the thicket.

But there was none.

This moment in the gospel account always pricks a particular string in my heart. It feels so personal, almost like a memory that I've lived. It wasn't until recently that I realized why. It's because this is the only moment in Jesus' entire journey toward the cross that I too have experienced. How often have I prayed this prayer to God, desperately asking for a way out. How often have you?

And when do these "Gethsemane prayers" come rising out of us? Much of the time, it is our response to some impending consequences that are rushing in as a result of our own choices. We know we need to face the music, but we still want to run and hide. The spirit indeed is willing, but the flesh is weak.

Our choices have consequences. And often, the last thing we want to do is face the results of our mistakes, our debts, our failures. "Please, God, give me another option. If there's any other way, bail me out of this mess. Find me an exit ramp."

And He did.

You see, our sin is the very reason that Jesus was in the garden that night, praying that prayer. The Savior of the world had lived a totally sinless life, yet He was about to endure the full spiritual penalty for the sins of all mankind. Knowing that we could never fully face the eternal consequences of our bad decisions, Jesus went willingly to the cross in our place.

Jesus knew what He had to do. He also knew there would be no ram in the thicket, because He was the ram. He was about to become the answer to all of the "If there be any way" prayers, past, present, and future. He was the way. The only way. For everyone. Forever. "I am the way and the truth and the life. No one comes to the Father except through me" (John 14:6). So for Him, there was no other way.

Then Jesus spoke the words on which history hinged. "Nevertheless, not my will, but yours, be done" (Luke 22:42 ESV).

With that, Jesus relinquished any hold to His own rights. He put His trust and His life in the hands of His Father. In that moment, He became the Lamb who would go willingly to the slaughter. He was saying to His Father, "I will accomplish this mission no matter the cost." In that moment He was looking across history at us and saying, "I love you *this much*."

That's where we often find ourselves in our own lives too.

This kind of plea to the Father isn't always a response to the consequences of sin. Sometimes it's a reaction to the struggles and hardships that naturally occur when we agree to follow Him completely.

Part of us truly desires to take that leap of faith and fully submit to the mission that God is whispering to our hearts. But the other part of us wants to take control and do our own thing. Or at the very least, do His thing on our own terms. And that part of ourselves can be loud. Really loud. Deep down we understand that the Lord's plan is ultimately the best direction for our lives. But when the path is covered with moments that will hurt, we cry out for deliverance.

In the gloom of the garden, Jesus exclaimed His love for His Father and for us. Even knowing that we may not love Him in return, He was willing to pass the point of no return. In the garden that night, with tears in His eyes, Jesus told His Father in heaven, "I surrender." And He said it for us.

"Father … not my will, but Yours be done" (Luke 22:42).

That can be our prayer too. It is by no means an easy one to utter, because it requires an enormous amount of trust. But when

He submitted to the Father's will on our behalf, Jesus demonstrated this kind of trust for all of us.

Today, we can bow before our Savior and offer up our lives to Him as a living sacrifice. He submitted to the unbearable consequences that were meant for us.

What would happen if you relinquished
your own rights and ways and submitted to Him?
Can you say, as Jesus did,
"Not my will, but Yours be done"?

Today, simply say to God, "I trust You."

DAY 31

FIGHT

GOD IS FIGHTING FOR YOU

THERE'S A LOT OF TALK ABOUT EVIL.
Where it comes from, why it's here, and why
God doesn't seem to be doing anything to stop it.
Just scan the headlines on any given day and you'll wonder
if there's any good left in the world.

A few months ago, my youngest son, Tate, was having trouble
sleeping in his own bed. Night after night, he'd come into my
room in the middle of the night, telling me he was scared.

I did all the things a Christian dad is supposed to do.
I talked to him, prayed with him, assured him that God was
with him. I even created a fake bottle of "monster spray" and

covered the room, just in case. OK, maybe that last one isn't a Christian dad thing, but I tell stories for a living, so that's what happens.

I wanted more than anything to assure my son that there was no such thing as monsters. That his fear was all in his head. But that wasn't true. There are monsters out there. Maybe not the one-eyed, big-toothed, blue variety that he'd imagined. But there are definitely monsters roaming around the world. And they will one day come after my son.

They will come in the form of people who will seek to discourage him. The monster of lust will disguise itself as love, hoping to lure him into its web. There are monsters of greed and sloth and shame and rage. And they will have one primary aim: to derail God's plan for my son and to keep Him from Jesus.

That's always been the Enemy's plan. From the first time that serpent reared its head in the garden of Eden with lies and accusations and shame, right up to the garden of Gethsemane, where he thought he could use betrayal and anguish and distraction to thwart God's plan of salvation. He doesn't stand a chance. But that doesn't stop him from trying.

The Bible tells us that "the thief comes only to steal and kill and destroy" (John 10:10 ESV). One of his go-to moves is to whisper lies into our ears. The Father of Lies loves to create a soundtrack in our heads and then put it on repeat.

You're not good enough.

You'll never measure up.

You'll always be like this.

Without a doubt, the Enemy is real. He is the author of fear and doubt. Abuse and bigotry and hate all stem from him. Vice oozes from his nature as freely as virtue comes from God.

From the beginning, the Enemy has been trying to frustrate the redemptive plans of God, and that's what he wants to do in your life. The good news is, we're not without hope in our battle against him.

The Bible says that "though we walk in the flesh, we are not waging war according to the flesh. For the weapons of our warfare are not of the flesh but have divine power to destroy strongholds. We destroy arguments and every lofty opinion raised against the knowledge of God, and take every thought captive to obey Christ" (2 Corinthians 10:3–5 ESV).

Destroy strongholds. Demolish arguments. Defeat the Enemy.

Jesus led the way in the garden of Gethsemane. In the shadows of the trees that night, there was much more happening than we could ever imagine.

As the disciples prayed with Jesus and Jesus prayed to His Father, something was happening behind the scenes. The forces of good were waging war against the forces of evil. Hope was wrestling with despair. Faithfulness was going face-to-face with apathy. Courage was locked in battle with cowardice. Jesus was setting the stage for the final defeat of the Enemy.

I love the scene in *The Passion of the Christ* when Jesus is in the garden and Satan comes to discourage Him, to tempt Him, just as he had in the wilderness three years earlier. In the movie, the Enemy takes on the form of a snake, and in the moment of the "Not my will, but yours" decision, Jesus steps on the head of the snake. Yes! That's my Jesus.

Today, when the Enemy comes against you and tempts you with arguments and opinions and ideas that are contrary to God's plan, you can do what Jesus did. Remind him that the battle has already been won. That Jesus defeated him two thousand years ago and that you are free.

Today, you can speak the word of God into your situation, whatever it may be. You can worship with abandon. And if you resist the Enemy, he will flee.

DAY 32

EAR

JESUS IS THERE TO PUT YOU BACK TOGETHER

THAT DAY STARTED LIKE ANY OTHER FOR MALCHUS. He woke up early, as always, to prepare to serve the high priest. That was his job as a servant, and he did as he was told. According to Jewish law, he was the property of the owner, who could buy or sell him at any time.

Malchus didn't have any aspirations of becoming a priest or rabbi or anything other than what he was. He'd been told his entire life that he amounted to little, that his life was not his own, that he belonged to someone else, that his life didn't really matter.

That night, when the high priest summoned him and told him that he wanted him to accompany a group of temple guards on a mission to confront a religious zealot named Jesus, Malchus anticipated a night of accusations, finger pointing, shouting, and eventually an arrest—just like always.

But something was different about this mission. To begin with, the guards were led by one of Jesus' own disciples, a man named Judas, who'd sold him out. And Judas led them, of all places, to a garden.

When they arrived, Judas stepped through the shadows toward the man from Galilee. Judas exchanged a kiss along with soft words Malchus couldn't hear.

As the guards moved toward Jesus, they fell face forward onto the ground, as if some invisible force had struck them.

Chaos ensued. Another disciple, perhaps seeing an opportunity for escape, lunged forward, sword drawn. As other men and soldiers pressed in, Malchus felt a hand in his back. With a jolt, he fell, toppling toward the man with the drawn sword. He felt a sensation like fire on the side of his head and cried out in overwhelming pain.

Tumbling to the ground, Malchus pressed his hand to his head. Blood dripped over his hand, down his arm, and onto the ground. The world around him grew blurry as he lay sprawled on the dirt, stunned. The noise around him became distorted, echoing as if he were in a cave. Then he couldn't hear anything.

His ear had been cut off! Malchus looked wide-eyed at the religious leaders, who were staring at Jesus.

Jesus was kneeling in front of Malchus, pulling something out of the dirt. His ear! Jesus placed His hand, now covered in blood, over Malchus's ruined head and held it there.

In that moment, everything stopped. There was no yelling, no moving, nothing. All stood still. It was as if heaven and earth had paused to witness this moment.

This man was no rebel.

A warm heat come over Malchus as he gazed into the eyes of Jesus. Jesus looked at him, into him, to his very soul. All that Malchus saw and felt was love. As if he were looking into the very eyes of God.

When Jesus took His hand away, Malchus heard a popping sound. He touched the side of his head where the wound had been. His ear was reattached. He had been healed.

In that moment, Malchus knew, for the first time, that he was loved, that he was noticed, that he mattered. For once, he wasn't kneeling down to pick up something for his master. The Master was kneeling to pick something up for him. The King had become the servant.

Even in the midst of His betrayal, Jesus stopped to show love, to heal, to remind a servant boy whom no one else noticed that he mattered.

Today, in the midst of the chaos of your life, the Savior sees you. You have not gone unnoticed by the Creator of the universe. You matter to Him.

But I'm not worth His time.

My issues aren't dramatic enough for Him to care.

Really? In the middle of the most volatile situation Jesus had faced up to that moment, He made Himself fully vulnerable to His accusers so that He could tend to the needs of a slave. He ignored everything else to step into Malchus's pain.

Why was Malchus so important? This is the only moment from his life that history has recorded as being of any conse- quence. Why would Jesus spend His final moments of freedom with this nobody? The answer is simple, though sometimes hard to grasp. In the eyes of the Savior, every one of us matters.

For the widower who feels the ache of aloneness, He is there.

For the teenager convinced that no one understands, He is there.

For the soldier who gave more than most but feels broken, He is there.

Jesus wants to mend the parts of your life that feel broken. No matter how small you feel, you are not invisible to God. Like a mother or father who gets up seven times a night to comfort a needy newborn, God will always give you His complete attention. You are not a nothing. You are His.

Take a moment to consider how incredible it is to have a Father who sees you and loves you unconditionally!

DAY 33

TRADED

JESUS WANTS YOU TO BE FAITHFUL

EVERY YEAR, THE NFL (AND NEARLY
EVERY OTHER PROFESSIONAL SPORT)
has a period of time when teams can trade
players or drop players from their roster. Every year,
fans watch closely, hoping to lose dead weight and pick up
a rising star. And every year, we see pictures of once-celebrated
heroes who have moved from the front page of the sports section to the back page of sports history in a matter of months,
sometimes weeks.

It's amazing how quickly we turn. One season we're cheer-
ing someone on and the next season we're booting them off

the team. On the Wheaties box one day and into the trash bin the next. The kid who dominated college sports finds himself in the big leagues, head spinning, and then the next thing he knows, he's working at AutoZone, wondering what happened to his promising career.

People are fickle. One day we love Starbucks; the next day we only drink "craft coffee." One day we think beards are only for lumberjacks; the next day, beards are for hipsters. People have always been easily swayed by the crowd.

I think that affected Jesus too.

After Jesus was arrested in the garden of Gethsemane, He was beaten and then shuffled between various religious and political leaders, each one playing hot potato, not wanting to sully their reputations by dealing with the potential political powder keg that was Jesus. Ultimately, Jesus ended up in front of Pontius Pilate, who quickly deflected any responsibility by leaving it up to the crowds to decide what to do with Him.[11]

One day Jesus was riding into Jerusalem with thousands of people on the streets, in windows, and in trees, all triumphantly shouting, "Hosanna," waving palm branches, and throwing down their cloaks on the road in front of Him. Talk about a hero's welcome. The people were ecstatic.[12]

Within a few days, the crowd turned on Him. The people who had called Jesus the Messiah when He multiplied the bread and fish were now calling for His death. The ones who'd waved palm branches were now shaking fists. The crowds who'd shouted in amazement when they saw Him heal the sick and raise the dead were suddenly shouting, "Crucify Him!"

Isn't that what we do? I know I'm guilty of it.

---

11   See Mark 14–15.
12   See Matthew 21:9.

When things are going well, I pump my fist, strike a Tim Tebow pose, look up to heaven, and holler, "Thank You, God!" But when things fall apart, or I sense that God is asking me for more than my fair share, I start to wonder if there's any way to trade in the old version of Him for a new one.

God is not Steve Jobs. Nor is he an iPhone. He doesn't offer us a newer version of Christianity just because the old version doesn't fit our expectations or meet our needs anymore. He doesn't hold an annual meeting to calm fears and address the naysayers and hope that the stock of Christianity is buoyed a bit as a result.

"Jesus Christ is the same yesterday and today and forever" (Hebrews 13:8). And He is looking for people who will worship Him, love Him, and serve Him regardless of how their situation changes.

So what will we do with Jesus? Will we turn on Him when things get uncomfortable? Will we trade Him out for a version that's easier to swallow, one that meshes better with our postmodern sensibilities? Or do we just shake our heads and keep our doubts to ourselves?

Jesus doesn't ask us to follow Him blindly or to go unthinkingly into the unknown. He loves it when we ask questions, when we complain, when we tumble around big ideas about theology and culture. And He's there when we cry out in frustration or desperation.

The Bible is full of men and women who were honest with God. The book of Jeremiah is sometimes referred to as "Jeremiah's Complaints." In one verse the guy is worshipping God, and in the next verse, he's wondering where God is. I can relate to that. Moses and Abraham asked honest questions too. And the disciples were constantly second-guessing.

God understands when we're gung-ho one day and angry with Him the next. It doesn't make Him nervous when doubt sneaks in. On the contrary, He loves it when we ask questions.

He asks only that we stay in the fight with Him, that we don't abandon Him when the heat gets turned up. That we don't toss Him out like yesterday's news. That we don't exchange the real Him for a version of Christianity that's more convenient or easier to explain away or less intrusive.

Faith is messy. It's supposed to be.

---

*Do you ever find yourself wishing you could
exchange the real God for a more palatable
version when times get tough, or when your
desires don't seem to line up with His timeline?
If so, meditate on Hebrews 13:6–8:*

*So we can say with confidence,
"The Lord is my helper; I will not be afraid.
What can mere mortals do to me?"
Remember your leaders, who spoke
the word of God to you.
Consider the outcome of their way
of life and imitate their faith.
Jesus Christ is the same yesterday
and today and forever.*

DAY 34

STRIPES

JESUS TOOK THE STRIPES FOR YOU

JESUS RECEIVED THIRTY-NINE LASHES ...
> For every time I turned my back on Him.
> For the secret sins I'd be horrified of in public.
> For the times I rejected the poor and hungry.
> For the holidays when I hurt the ones I love.
> For the way I judge people I know nothing about.
> For the days I think I can do it all on my own.
> For the e-mail that I wish I hadn't sent.
> For the e-mail that I wish I had sent.
> For the stuff I gathered but never needed.
> For the evenings I fell asleep mad at people I care about.

For the times I thought I was better than someone else.

For the pain I caused people who never saw it coming.

For the looks I gave that spoke a thousand unkind words.

For the mornings I woke up and decided to carry my own burdens.

For the envy I allowed to hollow out my soul.

For the excess that I secretly loved.

For the silence when I should have shouted.

For the shouting when I should have been quiet.

For the two faces I wore on too many days.

For the date when I went too far.

For the website that I lingered on for too long.

For the words that cut deep.

For the poor whom I ignored.

For the selfishness that I hide.

For the lust disguised as love.

For the lack of patience.

For the way I wasted precious time.

For the meals I overate because I was depressed.

For the people I refused to forgive.

For the ache of loneliness.

For the feelings of inadequacy.

For the addiction I can't kick.

For the laughter at another's expense.

For the times I only *acted* generous.

For the fear of failure.

For the fear of rejection.

For the fear of everything.

For hope.

For freedom.

For *love*.

DAY 35

UNKNOWN

EXPECT THE UNEXPECTED

WHEN I WAS TWELVE YEARS OLD, my dad bought a Winnebago camper and our family took a trip to Mexico. I liked to sleep in the bunk above the cab while my dad drove at night. I would watch the lights flicker by on the interstate and think about life and what lay ahead.

The RV created for us the Wild West of family vacations. Apparently there were no seat belt laws for RVs in the '80s, so my five siblings and I could spread out and stretch and use the bathroom without Dad having to pull over. My mom made sandwiches as we all sang '70s tunes, rolling down Highway 61.

I've always wanted to repeat that memory for my own family, so one summer I decided to go for it. I was working for myself and in the middle of a writing project, and I thought it would be fun to buy a used RV and spend a few months together as a family traveling the country.

What could go wrong?

As soon as we pulled out of the driveway, something felt weird. But I ignored the subtle warning. As we crossed the Ravenel bridge from Mount Pleasant to Charleston, the RV started to shake. Not a little shimmy. The thing rocked back and forth like a fishing skiff in the middle of a category 4 hurricane.

I pulled over to call my "RV guy" and asked him about it. Apparently, with all of our meal-making and bathroom use en route, we had put too much water into the holding tank.

"Welcome to driving an RV," he said. "You'll get used to it."

It took me a few tries to figure out how to empty the waste-water tank. But I finally managed, and we were on our way again. Sarah said, "Well, if that's the worst thing that happens, we'll be fine." We laughed.

But that was only the beginning. On that trip our headlights went out while driving down a mountain pass, a tire popped on the Continental Divide, we almost ran out of gas in the Badlands, and I was constantly repairing things.

Our "RV Summer" was filled with mishaps, near tragedies, and nail-biting moments. But it was also, to this day, the best vacation we've ever had. Every one of my five kids would tell you that. In fact, whenever we're feeling a bit disconnected as a family, one of the kids will say, "Sounds like it's time to buy an RV."

But if you ask the kids what they remember most about that trip, they won't talk about the line-dance contest as we drove through the Dakotas, cooking dinner as we rambled across

Minnesota, or the campfires and s'mores. It was learning to deal with the unexpected that has stayed in their minds the most.

The Bible is full of stories of the unexpected. Moses couldn't have guessed that he'd be standing between the Red Sea and an army of Egyptians. David wasn't planning to take on Goliath. Even Jesus seemed to find Himself in situations that allowed for a bit of improvisation. He was at a wedding when the wine ran out and in a meeting when the food ran out.

Learning to pivot when things don't go our way is part of life. In football, a quarterback sometimes calls an "audible" during a play in order to adjust to the other team. But being flexible means we have to learn not to let worry control us.

We can't see tomorrow. We don't know what the future holds. We can connect the dots of our lives looking backward, but not forward. And sometimes that's disconcerting. But this gives us an incredible opportunity to "let go and let God."

During our RV summer, we all knew that a potential problem (or an adventure, as I like to call it) was always just around the corner. If we had allowed the fear of potential problems to control us, it would have been a horrible vacation.

We often worry about things that never happen. Jesus tells us that it's useless to worry. "Which of you by being anxious can add a single hour to his span of life?" (Luke 12:25 ESV). Then He says that if God takes care of the sparrows, surely He can take care of us.

It's human nature to worry. We worry about our kids, about our parents, about our finances, and even about our favorite sports team. Worrying seems like a natural part of being human. But God doesn't want us to carry the burden of worry. He wants us to "cast our cares on Him" so we can enjoy the full life that He has for us.[13]

---

13   Psalm 55:22 and 1 Peter 5:7 NIV

Pray with me:

God, give me the courage today to trust in You.
Take worry away and allow me to walk in confidence,
knowing that You see me, that You care for me,
and that You won't leave me on my own.

• • •

Have I not commanded you?
Be strong and courageous.
Do not be frightened,
and do not be dismayed,
for the Lord your God is with you
wherever you go.

(Joshua 1:9 ESV)

• • •

DAY 36

ROAD

JESUS NEVER GAVE UP ON YOU

IN 1913, AN ADVERTISEMENT appeared in the *London Times* that read, "Men wanted for hazardous journey to the South Pole. Small wages, bitter cold, long months of complete darkness, constant danger. Safe return doubtful. Honor and recognition in case of success."

The advertisement was placed by the famous adventurer and explorer Ernest Shackleton. At first glance, the ad makes it seem that the mission was in jeopardy from the beginning. Shackleton understood that to find the sort of men he wanted, he had to appeal to their sense of risk and adventure. And it worked.

Shackleton was so sure of his success that even before he embarked on his journey, he sold the movie rights and even scheduled a book tour about the yet-to-be-taken voyage. This undaunted courage and determination may have been just what he needed when he hit hard times.

During one particularly dangerous point of the journey, when his ship *Endurance* became locked in ice, he and his entire crew almost perished. One day, he wrote in his journal, "I called on the other men that the sky was clearing, and then a moment later I realized that what I had seen was not a rift in the clouds but the white crest of an enormous wave."[14]

On the voyage, Shackleton and his men were pressed to the limits of human endurance. They faced starvation, sharks, freezing weather, sickness, and shipwreck. Not to mention a gigantic wave during a "perfect storm." But the promise to return, the promise he'd made to his family and the families of his men, kept him alive and pushing onward, determined to accomplish his mission.

Jesus had a mission much more important than discovering a new place or conquering a mountain. He had laser focus on accomplishing a mission that had begun long ago in one garden and had already led Him through another garden. He would finish the story in a final garden, adorned with trees not made by God, but by man.

Forty lashes was considered an execution under Jewish law. Jesus endured thirty-nine. Before the flogging, He had already endured being beaten. He hadn't slept in two days. He was dehydrated and exhausted.

His tormentors fashioned a crude crown of thorns and pushed it onto His head, which bled profusely. Then He was

14 Alfred Lansing, *Endurance: Shackleton's Incredible Voyage* (New York: McGraw-Hill, 1959).

forced to carry His own cross through the streets to Golgotha, a filthy place on the outskirts of the city, where criminals were executed.

If bets were being made, the odds would be that this man would be dead before He reached Golgotha. But Jesus was driven by a great sense of mission. With every step, He knew exactly why He was taking it. As blood from the crown on His head blurred His vision, He understood that His true kingdom was coming. Through pain and embarrassment and loneliness and insults, He held on to that purpose. No matter what, He would not fail.

In that moment, you came to His mind. He would go the distance for you.

If God had written down a job description for the position Jesus filled on the cross, it might have read, "Son wanted for hazardous journey to Earth. You will be paid nothing. You will have no home. You will be abandoned, rejected, and betrayed. Your life will be threatened from the day You are born. Safe return is assured, but will require You to die painfully. Success will render forgiveness, redemption, reuniting the children of God to their Father, and a new heaven and earth."

Today, when things get tough or out of control, remember that you can lean in to the one who bore all and endured all for you.

Don't give up. Don't give in.

Today, "may the Lord direct your hearts into the love of God and to the steadfastness of Christ"
(2 Thessalonians 3:5 ESV)

DAY 36

DAY 37

TREES

JESUS ALWAYS FORGIVES

IT WAS NO COINCIDENCE THAT Jesus was crucified between two thieves. Those two men hung in place of each one of us. The very definition of a thief is someone who's taken something they haven't paid for. That's us. We took freedom. We took grace. We took hope. What did Jesus do? Rather than make us pay our own debt, He paid it for us.

Jesus' sacrifice on the cross can be responded to in countless ways. It can be mocked, it can be trivialized, it can be ritualized. But it cannot be ignored. The cross demands a response.

Two thieves hung from the crosses on either side of Jesus, and each of them responded differently.

One thief, upon seeing the sign above Jesus' head that read, "King of the Jews," asked Him, "Aren't you the Messiah? Save yourself and us!" (Luke 23:39). As this man hung dying, he chose to use some of his precious final words not to confess to his crimes but rather to mock Jesus. Like the first Adam, this thief responded by challenging God.

The thief on the other side of Jesus responded, "Don't you fear God? ... We are punished justly, for we are getting what our deeds deserve. But this man has done nothing wrong." Then He said, "Jesus, remember me when you come into your kingdom" (Luke 23:40–42).

In that moment, in his own way, the thief was declaring the lordship of Jesus. He was basically saying, "I've made a wreck of my life. If there's any way, please forgive me and give me a second chance. If not in this life, maybe in the next one."

Jesus answered him, "Truly I tell you, today you will be with me in paradise" (Luke 23:43). Not only would Jesus forgive the thief, but He would make the sinner on the cross next to Him the first citizen of heaven.

What happened in that moment was one of the most dramatic pictures of grace we see in the Bible. It reminds me of another picture.

A few years ago, I went to New York City to go to the infamous McKee Story Seminar. The event was life-changing, and it rewired the way my company thinks about story. But that wasn't the most impacting thing about my trip to New York.

One night, with some time on my hands, I decided to wander onto Broadway and try to pick up some cheap show tickets. I scored a great seat for the Friday night showing of *Les Miserables*.

The story of *Les Miserables* is one of the greatest portrayals of grace and redemption in all of show business. It centers around the life of Jean Valjean, who, as a young man, stole bread for his family and was arrested and sentenced to a work camp. When he had finally paid his debt to society and was released from prison, he was taken in by a compassionate bishop who gave him room and board.

Quickly falling back into his old ways, Jean Valjean stole silverware from the bishop's dining room. The next morning, he was caught and questioned by police. When the bishop was alerted, he told the officers that he had given the silverware to Jean Valjean. And, he added, he'd also given the thief two candlesticks that he had "forgotten" to take.

Jean Valjean was left dumbfounded. Nothing in his life offered him a precedent for what had just transpired. Not only was he allowed to keep the stolen silverware with no punishment or consequence, he had been given *more*! For the first time in his life he had experienced grace, and he could not even begin to understand why.

After the police left, the bishop told Jean Valjean that he should use these gifts to start an honest life. He added that Valjean, in that moment, had become a totally new person. Because of grace, his identity had changed forever. He was branded with freedom.

In the last words that the bishop utters on stage, he looks at Valjean and sings, "God has raised you out of darkness. I have bought your soul for God."

When Jean Valjean fully realizes what the bishop did for him, he falls to his knees, sobbing, determined to live differently.

As I sat there in the Imperial Theater on Forty-Fifth and Broadway, tears ran down my face too.

The story of *Les Miserables* unravels like a beautiful tapestry of grace, hope, and freedom. But the picture that stuck with me most was that of Jean Valjean, on his knees, his heart full of thankfulness to the bishop.

Like the bishop, Jesus gives us more than we've bargained

for. He offers us not just forgiveness for our sins, but hope for a resurrection life while we are still living. Jesus offers forgiveness for the thief willing to surrender to His love and lordship.

In that moment after the thief asked Jesus to remember him in paradise, the layers of guilt and the slime of sin peeled off of the thief and were blanketed onto Jesus. The one who knew no sin became sin so we could be free. Every sin—not just of that thief, but of you and me and every person past, present, and future—came crashing down on the Son of God. The thick mud of sin covered the innocent Lamb of God. And the Father had no choice but to look away.

Jesus cried out, "My God, my God, why have you forsaken me?" (Mark 15:34 ESV).

But in the next moment, sin was crushed. Death was defeated. Shame was swallowed up in victory.

The thief is now covered in white. The pall of sin is gone. Where there were once scars from shame and secrets, he wears robes of righteousness. Where once there were chains of addiction and bondage, now there is absolute and complete freedom.

Think of the areas of your life that sometimes hold you captive and ask yourself, "Why?" Those whom the Son have set free are free indeed. Beginning right now, you can walk in the freedom that God offers through the resurrection of Jesus.

• • •

In him and through faith in him we may approach God with freedom and confidence.

(Ephesians 3:12)

• • •

DAY 38

HUMAN

JESUS UNDERSTANDS

JESUS WAS FULLY GOD. **Before He ever walked the roads in Galilee, He scattered the stars into space, split the Red Sea in half, and stood in the fiery** furnace with three Hebrew boys.

His disciples watched Him as He controlled the weather and caused food to mysteriously multiply in plain sight. He made the blind see, the deaf hear, and the lame walk. No question, He was God in sandals.

But He was also fully man. He understood what it meant to feel grief, to grow weary, and to get thirsty. In many ways, Jesus was nothing like you and me, yet in many other ways, He was just like us. John said, "The Word became flesh and made his dwelling among us" (John 1:14 ESV).

When news that his friend Lazarus was sick and dying, Jesus traveled several days, only to be greeted by Lazarus's sister, weeping and filled with grief. Jesus was too late. Lazarus had already died and been buried.

After comforting family and friends, Jesus paused in front of Lazarus's tomb. Just as many of us have done—standing by a gravestone with bouquets of flowers and misty eyes on birthdays and memorial days and Christmas Eves—Jesus stood in front of Lazarus's gravestone. And He wept.

The one who dug out the Nile River with His words wept. Tears of sorrow flowed down the King's cheeks and dripped to the ground. The ache of loss filled Him, as it has so many who have lost loved ones. He felt the sting, the hollowness, the deep ocean of despair.

Jesus probably walked more than ten thousand miles during the three years of His public ministry. That's an average of ten to fifteen miles *every day,* in flip-flops, in the scorching heat. Definitely not for the faint of heart. One day, after walking all day with His disciples, Jesus was "tired from the journey" and went to a well to sit down and rest. (See John 4:6.)

The designer of the gazelle and cheetah and camel was just plain tuckered out. He was out of steam, out of gas, out of energy. He didn't pop into town with a Dale Carnegie grin on His face and a jump in His step. He needed a break. He shuffled over to the well to take a load off and take some water in.

On those days when you don't have anything left for the kids or your husband or anyone else, Jesus understands. On the days when work has you stressed out and mentally exhausted, He gets it. On the Saturday mornings when all you can manage is to drag yourself to the coffee maker and then flop on the couch, He knows your pain.

As Jesus hung from the cross, He spoke words that have been used in powerful sermons for generations. "Father, forgive them, for they know not what they do" (Luke 23:34 ESV). This is one of seven phrases that Jesus spoke on the cross. Six of the seven phrases are the types of things God would say; the other is made of words that only a man would say.

The Word had become flesh. In this moment, Jesus' flesh was crying out. As He hung on the cross, bleeding and dying, His fragile skin blistering under the hot sun, He had one simple request. "I thirst" (John 19:28 ESV).

While Jesus was focused on His God-given mission, His humanness was still in full force. His lips and throat were burning and parched. He wanted something to cool down His body. A cup of water. A drink. A little reprieve from the heat of the sun and the tang of blood. Something to wash down the grit from the road and the bile from His stomach.

When life has come full-force at you and you need a break, Jesus understands. When all around is sadness and you just want to laugh again, He knows what you're going through. When you feel dry and empty and void of life or faith or hope, He gets it.

Jesus has been in the deepest trenches of human emotions and hurt and pain. He empathizes with all of it.

After Jesus wept for Lazarus, He stretched out His hand and the God part of Him took over. He commanded death to depart. Then He watched Lazarus walk out of the tomb.

On the cross, not long after He choked out the words "I thirst," He cried out, "It is finished" (John 19:30 ESV). Thirst was swallowed up in death, and death was swallowed up in resurrection life.

That's the way Jesus is. Fully human to embrace your world and fully God to transform it.

The next time you feel like there's no way God could understand your life, remember that while He's the immeasurable Creator, He's also the one who got tired, sad, and thirsty.

Pray with me:

Dear heavenly Father, thank You for understanding me.
You know my name, You know my needs,
and You know my heart. Help me to trust You
and to walk by faith and not by sight.

DAY 39

SUFFERING

SUFFERING CAN CONNECT YOU TO JESUS

GROWING UP IN AN EVANGELICAL HOME, I used to cringe whenever I saw a crucifix. For some reason, I couldn't understand why people would want to wear a cross with Jesus' damaged body still on it. Why not an empty cross? Or even better, an empty tomb?

I was young and ignorant. And relatively untouched by the deep well that comes with suffering.

But I'm older now. And I've walked through my own seasons of pain. Jesus on His cross is everything to me now.

Pain wears many faces. Sometimes it digs at us, burrowing

deep into our souls, numbing us from the inside. Sometimes it blankets us like a thick, wet fog. It can look like indescribable anguish. Or blinding, incomprehensible rage. Sobs, shouts, clenched fists, gasps for air. Even describing it seems to trivialize it.

Paul talked about the "fellowship of His sufferings" (Philippians 3:10 NASB). People who have suffered deeply all have one thing in common: a shared wound. Soldiers, Holocaust survivors, and ex-cons all have a sort of "fellowship of suffering." They all know what the others have been through. All it takes is a nod, a look in the eyes, a handshake. Words don't even need to be spoken.

I've never been to war, but I've experienced the fellowship of suffering. I've seen it in others' knowing eyes. I've felt it in the touch of their hands. The nods of acknowledgment of something we wished we didn't share. The blank, slack stare that cannot be reached. The incessant, uncomfortable talking and over-talking, as if that could change anything. Even the wild looks of rage and anger.

Perhaps you know this kind of loss too.

For some, suffering begins young. For others, it creeps in later in life.

Have you ever thought less of your faith, your godliness, your authenticity because of this pain? You wouldn't be the first.

In the latter part of His public ministry, Jesus became very popular, and He had trouble getting anywhere quickly. In Matthew 9, we read that He was very late responding to a request to pray for a sick young girl. So late, in fact, that she died before He got there.

Can you imagine the hope those parents had, knowing the Healer was coming to pray for their daughter? Maybe they'd seen Him perform miracles. Perhaps they'd witnessed the once-blind man jumping about and exclaiming that he could see. Surely there was hope for their daughter too. Hope that she would be saved from death.

But minutes turned into hours and she grew worse. With one final exhale, she was gone.

Shock. Anger. Disbelief. Fear. Suffering.

And *then* Jesus showed up. *What's the point? Why even come? It's too late now.*

Then He said, "The girl is not dead but sleeping" (Matthew 9:24 ESV).

Come on, Jesus. Look closely. It's obvious our daughter is not just asleep.

Jesus goes into the house and takes her hand, and she sits up. She is alive! The breath of life comes back into her. It comes back into her mother and father too. And those who are close by. They are all marked now. They have joined the fellowship of suffering. But more than that, they have experienced what it means for Jesus to come into their suffering. He entered every facet, every angle, every emotion. He beheld each individual in his or her raw, naked grief, and He brought life there.

First Peter 4:13 tells us to "rejoice inasmuch as you participate in the sufferings of Christ, so that you may be overjoyed when his glory is revealed."

This is the hope we have. That we can and will have life again. That there is hope of living. That there will be joy.

But even the joy will carry with it a new depth of understanding. A richness and complexity not found without walking through this place of suffering.

When you see someone suffering through fresh pain or grief, you will know why Jesus died on that cross. You will have joined with Him in His suffering. Ultimately, this brings fullness to our walk.

The cross is a reminder that Jesus is with us in every moment, the good and the bad. When we embrace suffering, He meets us there. And He promises that there will be life again.

Pray with me:

Lord, thank You for always standing beside me.
You provide me with a future full of Your love,
blessings, and guidance. I know that no matter how
bad things get, You will always be by my side.
I may not see You or feel You, but I know You
are here because Your Word tells me so.

DAY 40

ALONE

JESUS KNOWS WHAT IT'S LIKE TO FEEL ABANDONED

IN THE FALL OF 1995, I was working as a youth pastor in Colorado Springs. Every Wednesday night after our meeting, Sarah and I sat on the edge of the stage and talked with any teenagers who wanted to.

One night, a girl named Kelly (not her real name) sat down next to me and told me her story.

Kelly had grown up in a pretty normal home. Her parents went to church, her dad worked a "regular" job, and she had always been a happy girl. Until the abuse began. Then Kelly started to go numb on the inside. And she began cutting herself. With big tears rolling down her face, Kelly gingerly lifted her sleeve to reveal a patchwork of scars on her forearm.

"I just feel so alone," she sobbed.

Of course, Kelly isn't the first person to feel alone. The insidious darkness of loneliness floats like a fog over the world, seeping into our homes and lives and offices and schools. How many people have cried out in the darkness of isolation?

The single mother, her head hung over the kitchen sink in desperation.

The teenager, unsure of his identity, desperate for someone to pay attention.

The businessman who buys whatever he can in an attempt to fill the emptiness of his heart.

The pastor who can't find anyone he can confess to.

Where does the ache of loneliness begin? Maybe with a divorce or an accident or at retirement. Or maybe, like Kelly, the loneliness begins with abuse.

Does God really understand what it means to be alone?

Yes. He does.

The most anguished cry of loneliness in all of human history echoed off the walls of Jerusalem, across the Kidron Valley, and back to Calvary.

Dark clouds gathered. Thunder rolled. Cold wind whipped the hillside as the crowd huddled together. The religious leaders stood back, whispering and pointing fingers at the carpenter hanging naked from the rough hewn wood. Mercenaries knelt on the ground, gambling for the last of Jesus' earthly possessions. Most of His friends had already abandoned him. The only disciple still around was John, who stood with his arm wrapped around Jesus' mother.

The Son of God, the Cocreator of the universe, the Admiral

of heaven, hung bleeding and dying. And utterly and totally alone. There is no heartache in all of history that could compare.

The beatings He could endure. The mockings He could bear. The crucifixion itself, though torturous, was worth the pain. But being abandoned by His Father? That was too much. In that moment, Jesus cried out, "My God, my God, why have you forsaken me?" (Matthew 27:46).

The scapegoat for all of humanity was sent alone into the wilderness of loneliness, to carry away the sins of the world. For a moment, the Trinity ceased to exist. The circle was broken. Christ hung alone. The only one with enough divinity to bear the weight of humanity.

Why did Jesus have to be separated from the Father? Sure, there's theology to point to and prophecy to fulfill. But I think there's more. I believe Jesus hung alone and abandoned so that you and I and Kelly and everyone else wouldn't have to.

As I talked to Kelly on the edge of that stage, I told her she didn't need to hurt herself because Jesus had already endured the pain and taken the stripes for her. I assured her that she wasn't alone and that Jesus understood her because He had felt abandoned too.

I decided that day that my wife and I needed to tell—no, *show*—as many people as possible what Jesus endured for them. That was the day "The Thorn" was born. It was created to show anyone who watched it how deeply Jesus loves them and how He willingly endured the greatest pain in the universe, loneliness, so that we would never have to.

Have you ever felt alone? Do you feel like God cannot possibly understand the loneliness you feel? Even Jesus felt abandoned. But in reality, God never left His side.

He will never leave you either.

Pray with me:

Heavenly Father, I pray that You would be present with me even when I feel alone. Thank You for the way You've been there for me so many times in the past. I know that You will never leave me or forsake me.

• • •

I am convinced that nothing
can ever separate us from God's love.
Neither death nor life,
neither angels nor demons,
neither our fears for today
nor our worries about tomorrow—
not even the powers of hell
can separate us from God's love.
No power in the sky above
or in the earth below—
indeed, nothing in all creation
will ever be able to separate us
from the love of God that is
revealed in Christ Jesus our Lord.

(Romans 8:38–39 NLT)

• • •

DAY 41

JESUS FORGIVES YOU, ALWAYS

HAVE YOU EVER MADE A PROMISE only to break it before you even knew it? I can't count how many times I've stood on the scale, turned to Sarah, and said, "That's it. No more sugar." Usually, within fifteen minutes, I'm devouring one of her frosting-glazed blueberry scones. That's what I call steely discipline.

But there's always tomorrow, right?

That's often how it goes. We make seriously heartfelt resolutions.

Stop gossiping.

Start working out.

Schedule a weekly date night.

Don't drink too much.

Call my parents.

But before we've even given ourselves enough time to get into a groove, we quit. We give in. We fall off the wagon.

I've often thought that Peter was the disciple who was the most like me. Thomas was the doubter, the skeptic. John was like the teacher's pet. He even called himself "the beloved." Matthew was sort of like a former Jewish mafia turned good guy. But Peter was the everyman. Well intentioned but all too human.

I imagine Peter as a gnarly looking, hard-working fisherman, with calloused hands and permanent wrinkles in his face from the sun. Sort of the Marlboro Man of Galilee. When Jesus first met him, Peter had been fishing all night and was cleaning up his boat after getting skunked. Jesus offered him a bit of fishing advice by telling him to go back out and cast his nets over on the *other* side of the boat.

This would have been a seriously annoying moment for most people. I mean, Peter was a seasoned fisherman. While Jesus knew the value of hard labor, He was a woodworker, not a dock worker. And it wasn't like Jesus had handed Peter a secret lure or some new power bait. He merely told Peter to throw his nets on the other side of the boat. That would be like fishing all day and then someone telling you, "Why not try it with your left hand?" As if that's going to make any difference.

But Peter didn't mock Jesus or walk away from Him. Instead, he loaded up his boat again, rowed back out into the open water, and dropped his nets on the opposite side of the boat. And Peter caught so many fish that the nets began to break. Talk about abundantly more than you could ask or imagine (Ephesians 3:20).

After that, Jesus asked Peter to leave his boat behind and follow Him. Peter did it, seemingly without a second thought. He'd
seen Jesus in action and wasn't about to let the opportunity of a
lifetime pass him by. (See Luke 5:9–11.)

There's no question that Peter was a sold-out follower of
Jesus. That's why it's so hard to understand how Peter could deny
that he even knew Jesus. Yet that's exactly what he did. Shortly
after Jesus was arrested in the garden of Gethsemane.

Mark 14:43–72 tells us that when the Roman soldiers took
Jesus, the disciples quickly split, fading into the shadows, not
wanting to get arrested along with Him. But several of them,
including Peter, followed the soldiers to see what was going to
happen.

The first stop for Jesus that night was the house of Caiaphas,
the high priest.

With his heart pounding in his chest, Peter managed to sneak
into the high priest's courtyard and made his way to a fire burning
near one of the gates, where a small group of people had gathered.
He hoped to get a little warmth, but more important, to see if anyone had heard anything about the fate of Jesus. It didn't take long.

"Have you heard what happened tonight?" one of them asks.

"Yes. They arrested Jesus."

Peter is about to speak up when another person says, "Good.
I was always a little suspicious of Him ... and His *disciples*."

Peter pulls his cloak up so that it covers his head, shadowing
his face.

"What's the charge?" someone asks.

"Blasphemy."

Peter turns slightly to see if he can slip away. But the small
crowd is hemming him in, pinning him to the inner circle near
the fire. He tilts his head down.

"I hear Caiaphas is hoping for the death penalty," someone says. Peter's heart pounds harder.

"They should arrest His followers while they're at it," one man says. "Caiaphas needs to make a statement."

The crowd agrees with murmurs and nods. Peter's stomach turns and his mouth goes dry.

What is he doing here? He's a simple fisherman, not a hardened criminal. How is this even happening?

Peter feels a tug at his robe, and the cloak covering his head is pulled down. He nervously yanks it back over his head.

"Hey, I recognize you," someone says, pointing at Peter.

He looks away.

"Me too. He's one of Jesus' disciples."

"No, I'm not," Peter says, not believing the words that just tumbled out of his mouth.

"I'm sure of it," another person hisses. "You're one of them."

Peter is cornered. He feels his old temper kicking in. "You must be mistaking me for someone else."

A woman squints at him, her eyebrows drawn together. "No, I definitely recognize you. I never forget a face. You were with Jesus of Nazareth."

"No! I am not who you think I am. I don't know Jesus."

The small crowd grows quiet. A moment later, a rooster crows, three times. The haunting noise cuts through the night air like a knife.

A sudden well of emotion nearly causes Peter's knees to buckle. Anguish wracks him with the realization of what he's done—the very thing Jesus predicted. He's denied the one he swore to follow to the very gates of death.

In Peter's eyes, the crowd disappears. All he can see is the face of his Savior and friend.

Peter pushes his way through the crowd and runs from the courtyard, bursting into tears.

The next few days go by in a blur. Jesus is accused, flogged, forced to carry His cross to His own execution, and then buried in a rich man's tomb. The guilt is crushing.

The Bible doesn't say where Peter was on Sunday morning. Maybe he was with the other disciples. But when God the Father breathed life back into Jesus the Son and raised Him from the dead, blowing the tomb door off the wall, Jesus had a special message just for Peter.

When Mary saw an angel at the tomb, his instructions were simple. "Don't be alarmed." (Yeah, right.) "Go, tell his disciples and Peter" (Mark 16:6–7).

Jesus knew that Peter was drowning in self-loathing and guilt and shame. So He wanted to make sure that Peter, specifically, knew that Jesus didn't hold anything against him. He wanted Peter to know that He forgave him completely.

Jesus says the same thing to us. When we fail Him, when we fall off the wagon, when we make promises we can't (or don't) keep, He meets us where we are and sends us a message. That He understands when we mess up, when our character sags, or when we say one thing and then do another. And He always forgives.

Have you, like Peter, made promises to
God that you haven't kept?
Ask the Lord to show you His forgiveness today.

DAY 42

REGRETS

JESUS GAVE EVERYTHING WITH NO REGRETS

IN 1904, WILLIAM BORDEN, heir to the Borden milk fortune, was given a trip around the world as a graduation gift from his parents. On the trip, William saw firsthand the world's destitute and hurting people and was determined to become a missionary. When his friends questioned his judgment, suggesting that he would be *"throwing away his life,"* William wrote in the back of his Bible the words "No Reserves." It was his way of telling God that he was all in.

William went on to Yale, and while he was there he started a small prayer meeting that eventually grew to more than 1,500 attendees and sparked a revival at the school. Upon graduation, William was offered several high-paying jobs, all of which he declined. Focused on his vision for the poor, William boarded a boat for Africa and wrote the words "No Retreats" under the words "No Reserves" in the back of his Bible.

The young missionary stopped first in Egypt to learn Arabic. While there, he contracted spinal meningitis and died a short while later. The news of Bordon's untimely death traveled quickly, and newspapers around the world carried stories about the tragedy of a life wasted. When William's Bible was found, there were two final words written in the back.

Under the words "No Reserves" and "No Retreats" were the words "No Regrets."

Two thousand years before William set sail for Africa, a thirty-year-old from Nazareth hung up His carpentry apron for the last time. Leaving the family business, He was determined to follow His calling to "the least of these" (Matthew 25:40 ESV). Three years later, the carpenter lifted His weathered hands toward His Father in a moonlit garden and said, "Not my will, but Yours, be done" (Luke 22:42 ESV). There was no Plan B. This was it. He was all in.

No reserves.

For two days after that, Jesus endured unimaginable pain. He was betrayed by one of His closest friends. Another denied that he ever knew Him. The rest of His friends scattered and hid while He was beaten, mocked, and flogged. Pushed to the edge of human endurance, Jesus pressed on until there was nothing left. He laid it all out for us. He hung on a lonely hill, stripped naked, with no strength left, drained of tears, blood, and dignity, with no rescue in sight. He could have called thousands of angels to help Him (Matthew 26:53), but that was not the plan. Even as the nails were being driven into His hands and feet, He knew there was no turning back.

No retreats.

The Cocreator of the universe hung on the cross and bore the sins of everyone, past, present, and future. Even facing the jaws of death, Jesus did what only He could do.

He forgave.

He forgave the religious leaders snickering from the shadows. He forgave the soldiers gambling for His only remaining possessions, oblivious to God on the cross. He forgave the thief who hung beside him who was full of hate and accusations.

And then, at the end of Himself, His goal in clear sight, with one final breath, the Admiral of heaven cried, "It is finished" (John 19:30 ESV). Thunder clapped as heaven echoed with His final words.

Jesus paid the price for all of us. For every misstep and mistake and misgiving that we've made or ever will make. For every sin, every shame, every bondage. Jesus took it all.

No regrets.

After three short years of ministry, Jesus bled and died and gave His life for us, knowing He would soon plunge to the gates of hell and wrestle the keys to death away from the Enemy. Then He would rise again and bring with Him the power of the resurrection with which He would empower His church. He could not hold and heal and forgive more people. He commissioned us to walk after Him and finish the task.

No reserves. No retreats. No regrets.

Are you living a life of no reserves, no retreats,
and no regrets? If not, what small step
can you take today to begin?

DAY 42

DAY 43

TRULY

JESUS IS THE SON OF GOD

HAVE YOU EVER SEEN THOSE GUYS WHO DO CIVIL WAR reenactments? Or the people who dress up for Renaissance festivals? Or the attendees at Comic-Con, who dress up as Ewoks or Vikings or X-Men? I used to wonder how in the world someone could get people to do that. Not anymore.

In every city that "The Thorn" tours to, we recruit local volunteers to play some of the parts in the production. We look for townspeople, Pharisees, disciples, and centurions. Mostly men, of course.

We almost always have a tough time finding men who want to be part of the cast. I mean, how many men in the church will volunteer to be part of a drama in which they have to wear a skirt? But once we twist enough arms, the men we cast as centurions inevitably end up being some of the most committed members of our cast, coming back year after year.

Steve was one of those guys.

Steve served in the US Air Force for thirteen years. One Tuesday morning, he was at the Pentagon when an explosion hit. The compression from the blast sent him tumbling to floor, glass and walls and debris crashing around him.

Steve could see blue sky and smoke out of the crater-sized hole that had been blown out of the roof. People were screaming and crying and choking. He watched in horror as men and women jumped out of windows on the third and fourth floors. Others perished in the fire and smoke and wreckage. The most searing image for Steve was the face of the man who died in his arms.

That day in 2001, when a plane hit the Pentagon in Washington DC, 125 people died. Steve was grateful that he'd survived. But for a year, he was wracked with guilt that he'd lived while others around him had not.

For Steve, the experience of 9/11, compounded by a deep personal wound caused by a church leader when he was a child, drove him into a severe and deep depression. One day Steve locked himself in a closet with a gun in his hand, ready to take his own life. In utter desperation, he cried out, "God, if You're real, I will surrender my life to You forever. Please just take over."

Beginning that day, God began to reveal Himself to Steve. A few months later, he found a healthy local church. Soon after, someone invited him to attend "The Thorn." When the play was over, he sat in the auditorium for a long time, his heart reawakened to God's love. The following year, Steve volunteered to be in the production and was cast as a centurion.

Steve stood on the stage while the actor who played Jesus was being lifted onto the cross. Steve's job was to hammer in the nails. But suddenly, the actors and props and even the stage all disappeared, and Steve felt as if he were actually in the presence of Jesus. In that moment, Steve knew what the centurion in the Bible knew.

"Truly this man was the Son of God!" (Mark 15:39 ESV).

Suddenly, all the guilt and depression of 9/11 washed away. For the first time since he was ten years old, Steve felt whole again. He knew that he was worthy. And that made a tremendous difference in his life.

Each of us stands, like Steve, at the foot of the cross. Are you ready to surrender your life to the one who freely gave His for you? Maybe as you look at the trail of your life, you can see bright spots where you know Jesus protected you, carried you, or forgave you. And maybe you too can say, "Truly You are the Son of God!"

Ask the Lord to reveal to you the places in your life where He has carried, protected, and forgiven you. Write them down, remember them, and thank God for them.

Pray with me:

Dear Lord, thank You for protecting me and guiding me and calling me to You. I know that You have always been there for me, watching over me.

DAY 44

ALIVE

JESUS SHOWS UP WHEN YOU LEAST EXPECT IT

EARLY ON SUNDAY MORNING the disciples were huddled together. John and James spoke in hushed tones. Peter sat by the window, his hand pulling at his beard, his mind searching for answers. They were all there except Thomas … and Judas. Mary and Martha had left before sunrise to anoint Jesus' body.

Somber emotions. Long sighs. Anxious pacing. Forlorn looks. Exclamations under breaths.

"How could this happen?"

"I sure didn't see that coming."

"Now what are we supposed to do?"

The mood in the room was like a wake.

A banging at the door made them jump. Then tense up. No one spoke. Andrew motioned for everyone to be quiet. Peter shuttered the window, then walked to the door. "Who is it?" he whispered.

"It's us!" Mary said. The door opened, and she burst inside. "They have taken the Lord out of the tomb and we don't know where they've taken him!"

Even before she could get the words out, Peter and John raced toward the tomb, stumbling over rocks and ruts. Their hearts raced with a million emotions all at once.

John got there first but stopped short of the tomb. He reached down and picked up a scrap of cloth. It reeked of myrrh. A burial cloth.

Peter went inside the tomb, looking, turning over stones. He found the other grave clothes. But he didn't find Jesus. Maybe, in those moments, Peter and John wanted to believe that a miracle had happened, just as Jesus said it would. Or maybe they allowed doubt and fear to creep in. Had someone stolen the body? Were the Sanhedrin setting them up ... just like they had Jesus?

They returned to their hiding place, closing the door behind them. The other disciples were anxious to know what they'd seen. Mary kept saying that Jesus was alive. John held her, calming her as if she were a delirious child. Peter was pacing, and double-checking the sword at his side. He'd used it once this week and wasn't afraid to use it again.

Fear doubled down on the group. Doubt set its claws in. A few of the disciples started packing their bags. The party was over. Everything was falling apart.

And then, literally out of nowhere, Jesus appeared, as He often does in the midst of doubt and fear. When we feel like our backs are against the ropes and the Enemy is coming in for a final sucker punch. When our hope has drained out and all we want to do is run.

Jesus said, "Peace be with you!" (John 20:21).

What a great sense of humor Jesus has. He could have knocked, given them a warning, greased the skids a bit. I mean, this was a big one. He had risen from the dead. And not like Lazarus, who was sick and then died. (See John 11.) Jesus had been beaten, bruised, crucified. Everyone saw it. But instead of warning them, He chose to appear out of thin air.

Big eyes and dropped jaws turned to smiles and laughter as the disciples gave Jesus soldier-coming-home kind of hugs. Jesus had come back to make all things right again. He had kept His promise. Of course He had. How could they have ever thought otherwise?

But we do. We know that Jesus came to bring us life. And yet we pace and wonder and allow fear and doubt to creep in.

Will my son ever come home?

Will our lives ever return to "normal"?

Will I ever get healthy?

Will I ever be able to shake this loneliness?

Listen. Do you hear that? There's a banging at the door of your heart. It might be the voice of a loved one or a friend telling you that Jesus is alive. That He has returned from the dead to crush the power of the Evil One. Trust them. Run with them and see for yourself. Find the empty grave. Know that He is alive. His promises are true. They don't always happen the way we want or when we want, but He's always faithful.

"Behold, I stand at the door and knock. If anyone hears my voice and opens the door, I will come in to him and eat with him, and he with me" (Revelation 3:20 ESV). Give thanks. Have hope. Trust Him. You never know when He'll show up out of nowhere and change everything.

In what ways has Jesus shown up unexpectedly in your life? In what ways do you need Him to show up today? As you go through your day, keep a keen eye out for unexpected encounters. Jesus might be trying to get your attention in ways you never imagined.

DAY 45

HOLES

JESUS GIVES YOU ROOM TO ASK QUESTIONS

THERE ARE TWO KINDS OF PEOPLE IN THE WORLD: those who read labels and those who don't. My dad is a label reader. When I was a kid, going to the store with him was nearly an all-day affair. He had to read *every single* label.

He wanted to know what was in that product, what it was supposed to be used for, and what it claimed about itself. How many ingredients were in it? Was it "all natural"? Then he'd pick up the competitor's product and do the same thing, comparing the two until finally, sometime near the end of the world, he made his decision.

As I'm getting older, I'm becoming more and more like my dad. I can't tell you how many times I've been in the grocery store, debating over two different things, reading labels and comparing notes, until finally caving and calling my wife to get the verdict.

"Do you need diced olives or sliced olives? Do they have to be organic? What's the difference between whipping cream and heavy whipping cream? Did you want scallions or green onions?"

Living in the advertising age, we are used to labels. It's how we sell nearly everything.

World's best coffee

#1-rated SUV

Sexiest man alive

America's team

Unfortunately, our love affair with labels has translated to the way we see people too.

Jock.

Loser.

Slut.

Nerd.

Often, even the people we love the most and the ones who are supposed to love us jokingly put labels on us. When we want to put a little endearment on a label we've assigned to someone, we call it a nickname.

Some nicknames are great: Bruce Springsteen is "The Boss," Frank Sinatra was "Ole Blue Eyes," and Jack Nicklaus is "the Golden Bear." But imagine being called Scarface or Dr. Death or Slick Willie. Good or bad, labels have a way of sticking to us.

The disciples got nicknames too. John was called "the beloved" and Peter "the Rock." But imagine being called "Doubting Thomas." Of course, the Bible never calls him that.

But we've been attaching that label to him for the past two thousand years.

For reasons we don't really know, Thomas wasn't in the room with the disciples when Jesus first showed up. He sure heard about it, though.

"Thomas, you should have been there!"

"It was amazing!"

"You really missed out, man."

A week passed between the time when the other disciples first saw the resurrected Jesus and the day Thomas finally saw Him. I wonder what Thomas was thinking during those seven days. Did he feel left out? Did he wonder if the rest of the guys were making the whole thing up? Did he feel like he was on the outside of an inside joke?

Have you ever felt like everyone around you is experiencing something that you're not, especially when it comes to things of faith? Have you ever wondered if maybe God just passed you by? Or maybe you've wondered if everyone else is just a little bit delusional … or too gullible.

Whatever Thomas was thinking, Jesus knew it. And for reasons that only Thomas would really understand, Jesus made him sweat it out. But He didn't leave Thomas out for long. A week later, in the same room, in the same dramatic way, Jesus appeared again. But this time, it was just for Thomas.

Just as He did for Peter, Jesus made a special effort to communicate specifically and personally to Thomas that He loved him and that He wanted to be real to him.

What happened next is where Thomas gets the bad rap. When the disciples first told him that Jesus was alive, Thomas was skeptical, saying that he'd need to see the holes in Jesus' hands and side before he'd believe. But when Jesus showed up for Thomas,

He didn't judge him for not believing. He didn't berate him for his lack of faith. Instead, with what I imagine was a sly smile and a gleam in His eye, Jesus walked over to Thomas and said, "Put your finger here, and see my hands; and put out your hand, and place it in my side." Then I think He paused before He said, "Do not disbelieve, but believe."

Thomas fell to his knees and said, "My Lord and my God!" (John 20:27–28 ESV).

I think what Jesus said, or at least implied, to Thomas was "I know you have questions. Things don't come as quickly to you as they do to others. You want to see some proof before you believe. And that's OK. In fact, I made you that way."

That doesn't make Thomas a doubter. No, I think Jesus would have given him a different nickname.

Thinking Thomas.

Rational Thomas.

Careful Thomas.

What labels have others put on you? What does God say about you? Today, God wants to rip off the negative or hurtful labels that other have assigned to you and replace them with His own.

As the Author of life hung bruised and bleeding on a wooden cross, He took upon Himself all of the labels that others have put on you or that you've put on yourself. And in exchange, He gives you the same labels that the Father gave to Him. He says:

You are not abandoned; you are a child of God.

You are not ugly; you are beautiful.

You are not worthless; you are precious.

You are not condemned; you are forgiven.

You are not forgotten; you are seen by God.

Beyond anything you could imagine, you are loved.

Pray with me:

*Lord, show me the ways I have allowed
others or myself to put labels on me.
Today, I determine to break the power
of the negative words spoken over me
and I accept Your word about who I am.
I am forgiven. I am accepted.
I am precious. I am loved.*

DAY 46

GOD USES YOUR BROKENNESS FOR HIS GLORY

A FEW YEARS AGO, I HAD THE PLEA-SURE OF VISITING the British Museum of Art. I especially enjoyed walking through an exhibit that showcased Japanese art. There were paintings and tapestries and sculptures. And lots of pottery. As I wandered through endless hallways filled with pottery, I came to one room where each pot was secured carefully behind special glass. These had to be really valuable.

Maybe they were older than the other pots. Or they'd been owned by a dynasty or were made of expensive materials. As I looked closer, I realize that they all had one thing in common. They were broken, or at one time had been broken. And each of the vessels in that special room had been glued back together.

I didn't understand what made them so valuable until I read about kintsugi. In Japanese culture, the art of kintsugi, or the mending of broken pots, is considered one of the highest and most valuable of all artisan skills. Where most people would want damaged things to have hidden repairs and be made to look new, kintsugi follows a different philosophy.

Rather than covering up the damage, kintsugi incorporates the damage into the beauty of the restored item. The Japanese believe that the brokenness of an object is part of its history and should be celebrated rather than covered up. Kintsugi uses gold, silver, platinum, and other precious metals to fill in the gaps of the broken piece, resulting in something even more beautiful than the original.

That's exactly what God does for us. He doesn't cover up or hide our brokenness. Rather, He uses it to show His faithfulness in our story. We could call the broken lines in our lives our testimony. I know many people who reflect God's beauty all the more because of their brokenness.

Over the years, the students from Compassion International have told their stories many times as part of "The Thorn." Many share how God brought them out of poverty and human trafficking and fear and put them back together again as only He can.

My dad went through a decade of loneliness and separation from family, only to be drawn back because of the enduring love of God.

Jacob wrestled with God and walked with a limp for the rest of his life, a reminder of his brokenness and the way God met with him in the middle of it.

Jesus was the greatest example of beauty in brokenness. When He rose from the dead, He could have chosen to have a perfect body. And yet He chose for His resurrected body to bear the wounds of His brokenness. I think He wanted to show Thomas, and us, that there's something special about how He repairs broken things.

In our culture, we often want to cover up and airbrush out our imperfections. We want to put on a pretty face and hide the real us from the world. Facebook, Instagram, and Pinterest feed our insecurities and our desire to hide our messy selves. But what if the world around you needs to see your mess in order to see Jesus?

The most valuable part of the art of kintsugi is the precious metal that's used to connect the broken pieces. God is the glue that connects all the painful, broken, unattractive pieces of us and makes us whole. (See 2 Corinthians 4:7–12 ESV.) By covering up our stories, we inadvertently cover up the God who redeemed us and put us back together again.

Are you allowing God to shine through
and mend your broken pieces?
Have you hidden your pain out
of shame rather than allowed
God to be glorified in your brokenness?
Today, in your weakness, let Him be strong.

DAY 47

EYES

JESUS IS THERE EVEN WHEN YOU CAN'T SEE HIM

AS WE WALK ALONG in our faith journey, I think we all lose sight of Jesus from time to time.

In some moments, He feels close, like a good friend who visits with no warning. The one you can sit with for hours on the back deck, coffee in hand, leaning in to hear every word. The friend with whom you can be yourself, in sweat pants with no makeup. The sort of friend who doesn't need "warming up" before you dive into matters of the heart.

But sometimes, Jesus doesn't feel very close. All we get are glimpses of Him, in fits and starts, like He's hiding behind the clouds. Or like an old AM radio station that crackles, becomes crisp for a moment, and then goes to static. On such days, it's easy to wonder if we really know Him at all, or if He truly cares about our mundane, soccer-games-and-dinner-dishes lives. I mean, He's got bigger fish to fry, right?

I love the story of the two men on the road to Emmaus as told in John 24:18–35.

The big Passover celebration in Jerusalem was over and the cleanup had begun. It was like the ending to the Super Bowl. The streets were emptying and the Jerusalem version of the guys with long-handled claws were picking up what was left behind. Things had started getting back to normal, but conversations about the big event remained.

On the road to Emmaus that morning, two men were walking down the road, talking about all the things that had happened over the weekend. They had apparently rubbed shoulders with the twelve disciples and perhaps even been in the room when Mary came running back from the tomb.

Along the way, they were joined by a man whom I imagine to be cloaked like Luke Skywalker in *Return of the Jedi*.

It was Jesus in disguise.

As the men continued to talk about the crazy events in Jerusalem they'd just witnessed, the stranger asked what they were talking about. Flabbergasted, one of the men said, "Are you the only one visiting Jerusalem who does not know the things that have happened there?" (Luke 24:18).

"What things?" Jesus asked. I love how playful and coy He seems in this moment. Whoever thinks that Jesus had a stern face and a serious look all the time needs to read the Gospels!

"Don't you know about Jesus of Nazareth?" the man asked.

For the next hour or so, the three men discussed the Scriptures and the Messiah and the fulfillment of prophecy. After seven miles, they arrived at their destination and asked Jesus to join them for dinner. He agreed, so they sat and talked some more, probably laughing and telling stories. At some point during the meal, Jesus took bread, gave thanks, broke it, and handed it to them.

In that moment, their eyes were opened and they recognized Him. And then He disappeared from their sight.

That's what He does with us sometimes. One minute we're wondering if He's real, so we search the Scriptures and talk to friends and tumble around questions in our minds, which He loves for us to do. The next minute, He's as real as the person across the room from us. And then—poof!—He's gone.

I love what the men said after the original "disappearing act." They looked at each other in astonishment and said, "Were not our hearts burning within us while he talked with us on the road and opened the Scriptures to us?" (Luke 24:32).

That's how Jesus works. At times, He will sit on the side of the Sea of Galilee or on your back porch. You'll feel Him, see Him, know that He is all that He says. But at other times, He stirs things up and then puts on His invisibility cloak so we can't see Him. In those moments, He is just as close as always, but He wants us to search for Him. In His Word, in our friendships, in His church. Rest assured, He hasn't gone anywhere.

Stop and listen to your heart. Can you hear it crackling? Can you feel it burning? Jesus wants you to seek after Him.

• • •

You will seek me and find me
if you seek me with all your heart.

Jeremiah 29:13

• • •

DAY 48

HELP

JESUS MEETS YOU WHERE YOU ARE

WHEN WE THINK ABOUT CHURCH, WE MOST OFTEN THINK about a pastor teaching the Bible or a worship leader singing praise songs. But the church, at its core, has always been about a lot more than that. Church is the place where we get to be the hands and feet of Jesus to one another and to the world.

In the amazing diversity of God's church, we sometimes find beauty in the most unsuspecting people. Jerry was one of those people.

I met Jerry on a Sunday morning at the information counter

at my church, where he and his wife, Georgia Lee, had volunteered for as long as anyone could remember. Jerry had become something of a permanent fixture in the lobby at my church. And a bit of an imposing one at that.

If his white hair, suit jacket, and barrel chest weren't intimidating enough, the fact that he was a veteran of the Korean War was. Jerry reigned over the information booth from a swivel office chair like a monarch atop his throne. He only got up to address you if you were over the age of fifty and were respectful enough to dress up for church.

Apparently, I failed on both accounts that day, and Jerry let me know it. Regardless, I had volunteered to work behind the information counter, so I wasn't about to leave. Clearly there wasn't enough room in that town for both of us, so it was time for a showdown.

For reasons I still don't understand, instead of talking to Jerry about suits or ties or church information, I asked him about fishing.

I don't know why I thought he knew anything about fishing. But he did seem like the sort of guy who would. Turns out I was right. Jerry knew a lot about fishing. And that bridge allowed our worlds to connect.

For the next few months, I met Jerry behind the information counter every Sunday, and every week we talked about fishing. Eventually that led to conversations about life and business and family and his weak knees. We swapped fishing stories and predicted the scores of upcoming Broncos games.

Then a series of events began that ended in a way I could have never imagined.

Sarah and I were down to just one car for our family of seven. So for a few long months, we all piled into my vehicle, squishing together, limbs dangling everywhere. This took "Mom, she's in my space" and "He's breathing on me" to a whole new level. Needless to say, we needed another car.

One Sunday Jerry walked into the information booth and handed me a set of keys. "Here, this is for you."

"What do you mean?"

"You said you needed a truck, right?"

"Well, yeah, but I didn't mean … How much do you want for it?"

"What?" Jerry looked offended. "Nothing. It's yours. Do whatever you want with it. Keep it, sell it, whatever. It's right out there." He pointed to the parking lot. "I put on new tires and replaced the leather seat and had the oil and brakes done. Just change the oil every three thousand miles and it'll last you forever."

I walked outside the church and saw a beautiful white Ford F350 pickup sitting there. I think that's when I saw Jerry smile for the first time. He ambled up into the driver's seat and showed me all the bells and whistles of the truck as if he were the greatest car salesman in the world. We walked around the vehicle and he pointed out the only dent—one in the tailgate from a time he forgot to lower the gate when connecting his fifth-wheel camper.

"What do you think?" he asked.

"I love it."

It was perfect. A classic truck with a bunch of miles on it. Looked great from a distance but a little beat up from wear that you only noticed once you got close to it. Just like me.

As I drove my new diesel monster truck home, towering above everyone else on the road, I thought about my friendship with Jerry. This was exactly what church was for. A middle-aged guy with five kids trying to figure out life and an older man with so much generosity and love and tenderness pent up in his heart that he just needs someone to unlock it so it can come bursting out.

And all it took was a little talk about fishing.

Isn't that what Jesus had in mind when he founded the church? (He did start it with a handful of fishermen, after all.) After Jesus rose from the dead, He appeared to His disciples along with about five hundred other eyewitnesses. Before He ascended back into heaven, He gave some final instructions to His followers. We call it the Great Commission. I can picture Jesus standing on the hillside after the resurrection and saying to His followers, "Go and make disciples of all nations" (Matthew 28:19).

When He said that, He was essentially saying, "I'm leaving soon, so now it's your turn." For three years, Jesus had been the one who comforted the brokenhearted and healed the sick and helped the poor. Now He was counting on His church to be His hands and feet, His eyes and ears and mouth.

Jerry did that for me. He was God's voice, reminding me of God's faithfulness. He was God's hands, giving more than I ever expected.

Now it's your turn. You get to be Jesus to the world, just like Jerry was to me. Those hands of yours are His hands. Those feet are His. Those eyes are His too.

Pray with me:

God, give me Your heart for the lost,
the poor, the brokenhearted. Let me be You
to a hurting and broken world. Amen.

DAY 48

DAY 49

NEXT

WE NEED TO PASS IT ON

ALL OF MY LIFE, I'VE CONSIDERED MYSELF A PRETTY PROGRESSIVE GUY. I stay on top of the news. I usually know which are the best movies to see. I like to believe that I know what's in style. And I've always prided myself as being a "techie" of sorts.

I've recently come to realize that those days are gone.

I used to rule our home as the resident tech nerd. If something was broken, I was the one to call. If there was a problem with something electronic, just ask Dad to fix it. If you had a computer issue, you knew where to go.

But recently all of that has changed. I know things change for all of us as we age, like losing hair and getting dentures and suddenly liking lima beans. But I didn't see old age coming. I suppose I just never thought it would happen to me.

Turns out my son Harrison is a genius. I know every parent says that about their kids, but this boy is something else. He loves computers and electronics and video games and is about the closest thing to Steve Jobs I've ever known. He loves to take things apart and put them back together. He knows how to write software and even has clients across the world who found him on the fiverr.com website.

Now he's the one everyone asks to fix things. Our friends call him to reprogram their computers and install home stereo systems. I can't tell you how many times I've been sitting at my computer, totally frustrated about something, only to have Harrison walk up, punch a few keys like an airline ticket counter attendant, and *bam!* Problem solved.

I taught Harrison all that I could about computers and electronics and video games. Now it's his turn to lead the way. It's time to pass the tech-genius baton to my son. Granted, that's not a hard baton to pass.

The Bible is full of examples of the importance of the hand-off.

In the Old Testament, Jacob passed the baton to his son Joseph (Genesis 49:22).

Moses empowered Joshua to step into the Promised Land (Joshua 1:1).

Elijah gave Elisha his cloak, along with a "double portion" of his anointing (2 Kings 2:14).

Jesus understood the importance of empowering others and then getting out of the way. While He touched thousands of people during His ministry, He only personally invested in twelve guys.

He knew He wouldn't be around forever and He wanted to empower the "next generation" to do even greater things to build God's kingdom than He had done (John 14:12). And this is the Son of God talking!

The apostle Paul modeled the importance of leadership and empowering others in his friendship with Timothy.

While it's easy to say, it's a lot harder to do. It's tempting to try to maintain our influence rather than give it away. It seems easier to hire people who could never "surpass" you, but that doesn't set you up for long-term success.

When I think of the incredible time that we're living in, I wonder what the next generation will be capable of doing to bring the light of God's love to the world.

Technology is advancing faster and faster every year. Someone has invented a device the size of a dorm room refrigerator that can purify any form of liquid into enough clean water for a village in Africa. There is more and better information available today than ever before. A Masai warrior with a smart phone can know more today than the president of the United States could in 1975.

Today we have the privilege to see a new generation be equipped and sent out to impact our culture and the world in ways their parents never could. Rather than criticizing the next generation, we need to "fan into flames" the gifs of God in them (1 Timothy 1:6). Encourage them as they dream big.

Imagine the things that the next generation can accomplish if we disciple them, give them the tools, and send them out?

There are industries to transform.

There are works of art to be created.

There are governments to be led.
There are diseases to be cured.
There are people to be freed.

---

*Do you have people above you on the
"mountain of God" who are pulling you up?
And do you have people below you whom you're
lifting up and preparing to take the baton?
If not, find them.
If so, take time this week to meet with them,
to help them dream, and to encourage them to
continue to develop God's gifts in them.*

Are you ready to pass the torch?

DAY 50

WHERE DO YOU GO FROM HERE?

I WROTE THIS BOOK WITH FIFTY CHAPTERS because there were fifty days between the day Jesus ascended to heaven after the resurrection and the day God sent the Holy Spirit to energize His church. Whether you've read one entry every day for fifty days, or binge read, or picked the chapters that looked the most interesting to you, I hope you can walk away from reading this book with a deeper sense of God's love for you. I hope the stories within these pages have encouraged you as you walk out to live your own story.

Take a few moments right now to remind yourself of the things God told you as you read this. You might even want to write some of them down. Here are a few things I'd like you to remember:

God had you in mind even before the existence of time and space. He wove you from the fibers of life, carefully depositing in you a mind, body, and soul that was unique. You didn't just happen; you were designed. With more care than a brain surgeon and more detail than a master painter.

Even during times of silence or struggle, God is there. Just as He was there for the people of Israel when they were slaves in Egypt and when they wandered in the desert. When we least expect it, He shows up. Even when He's quiet, we can know that He hasn't left us.

Just when we think He's not there, His voice cuts through the silence. He invades our lives in ways we never expect, just as He did in Bethlehem on the first Christmas. He loves to show up in the middle of our messy lives.

God works in ways that defy the way things have always been done. He forgives when others write us off. He heals us when others want to hide us. He takes time for us even when we haven't given Him any room.

He walks on water so we'll have faith to do it too (Matthew 14:22–33).

He multiplies bread so we'll know that there's always more where that came from (John 21:13).

He made Himself like us so we would know He understands (John 1:14).

He endured the cross so we wouldn't have to (Hebrews 12:1–3).

He rose from the dead so we could live resurrected lives, even today (John 5:9).

He sends us out so that we can let His light and love rub off on a world that desperately needs Him (Matthew 5:14).

DAY 50

The story of God weaves itself across time, dipping into history and winding itself around our stories. The stories in this book represent only a small fragment of the stories that are told in the Bible. And the stories in the Bible represent only a small part of the whole of God's story. John writes that "Jesus did many other things as well. If every one of them were written down, I suppose that even the whole world would not have room for the books that would be written" (John 21:25).

My final challenge to you is to dig deeper than ever before. Seek answers to the questions that are burning inside you. Tumble around the stories in the Bible. And look for hints of God all around you.

Maybe you want to know God in a deeper way. God says that whoever seeks Him will find Him (Jeremiah 29:13). God isn't pushy. He doesn't force His way into our lives. He waits for us to look for Him. But trust me, He's waiting. God loves you so much that He not only gave His life, but He's willing to wait for you to look for Him.

Above all, remember that no matter where you are, no matter what you do, you will always be *so loved*.

• • •

In all these things we are more than conquerors through him who loved us. For I am sure that neither death nor life, nor angels nor rulers, nor things present nor things to come, nor powers, nor height nor depth, nor anything else in all creation, will be able to separate us from the love of God in Christ Jesus our Lord.

(Romans 8:37–39 ESV)

• • •

A SHOW LIKE NO OTHER

You can experience the power of The Thorn production live! Featuring live music, dance, aerial acrobatics and special effects, The Thorn presents the Story of God like you've never seen it before. Catch the National Tour at a location near you.

VISIT **THETHORN.NET** FOR
TOUR DATES AND LOCATIONS.

BRING HOME THE THORN

Experience the power of The Thorn with your friends and family with the live DVD recording! Pick up your copy today at **TheThorn.net**.